Everyday Spelling

Authors

James Beers • Ronald L. Cramer • W. Dorsey Hammond

Scott Foresman
Addison Wesley

Editorial Offices: Glenview, Illinois • New York, New York
Sales Offices: Reading, Massachusetts • Duluth, Georgia • Glenview, Illinois
Carrollton, Texas • Menlo Park, California

1-800-552-2259
http://www.sf.aw.com

ACKNOWLEDGMENTS

TEXT

page 10: "Big" by Dorothy Aldis reprinted by permission of G. P. Putnam's Sons from *All Together* by Dorothy Aldis. Copyright 1925–1928, 1934, 1939, 1952, renewed 1953–1956, 1962, 1967 by Dorothy Aldis. **page 81:** "The End" from *Now We Are Six* by A. A. Milne, illustrations by E. H. Shepard. Copyright 1927 by E. P. Dutton, renewed © 1955 by A. A. Milne. Used by permission of Dutton Children's Books, a division of Penguin Books USA Inc. and Reed Books. **page 107:** "Yellow" from *One at a Time* by David McCord. Copyright © 1974 by David McCord. By permission of Little, Brown and Company. **page 133:** "I Would Like to Have a Pet" from *Something Sleeping in the Hall* by Karla Kuskin. Copyright © 1985 by Karla Kuskin. Reprinted by permission of HarperCollins Publishers. **page 159:** "What is a family?" from *Fathers, Mothers, Sisters, Brothers* by Mary Ann Hoberman. Copyright © 1991 by Mary Ann Hoberman. Reprinted by permission of Little, Brown and Company. **page 185:** "Keziah" by Gwendolyn Brooks from *Bronzeville Boys and Girls* by Gwendolyn Brooks. Copyright © 1956 by Gwendolyn Brooks Blakely. Reprinted by permission.

ILLUSTRATIONS

pp. 3, 7, 9, 14, 22, 28, 34, 40, 46, 52, 57, 144, 148–149, 156–157, 161, 243–256: Lou Vaccaro; **pp. 3, 12, 17, 23, 35, 41, 47, 53, 59, 105, 195–196, 206:** Paul Harvey; **pp. 4, 66–67, 72, 78–79, 197–198, 217–218:** Cary Pillo; **pp. 4, 74–75, 81, 83–84, 117, 119, 122, 127, 131, 135, 140, 165, 192, 203–204, 215–216, 219–242:** John Sandford; **pp. 5, 91–92, 94, 104, 106, 111, 113:** Brian Karas; **pp. 5, 18, 24, 30, 36, 42, 48, 54, 60, 95–96, 99–101, 103, 110, 112, 166, 191, 201–202:** Elizabeth Allen; **pp. 6, 9, 133–136:** Jean Pigeon; **pp. 7, 152, 163–164:** Kate Gorman; **pp. 8, 141–142, 174, 179:** Suzanne Snider; **pp. 8, 115–116, 120, 184:** Mike Muir; **pp. 11, 19, 25, 31, 37, 43, 49, 55:** Lane Gregory; **pp. 13, 21, 27, 33, 39, 45, 51, 58, 207–208:** Anita Nelson; **pp. 20, 26, 29, 32, 38, 44, 50, 56, 171, 175, 182, 190:** Cheryl Roberts; **pp. 65, 69, 73, 77, 78:** Jean Cassels; **pp. 65–256** (pandas): Georgia Shola; **p. 67:** Thomas Penna; **pp. 68, 80:** Laura Cornell; **pp. 70–71, 85–88, 199, 211–212:** Susan Spellman; **p. 71:** Chi Chung; **pp. 76, 170:** Patricia Kutsch; **pp. 82, 138–139:** Dolores Johnson; **pp. 89–90:** Kirsten Soderlind; **pp. 93, 123, 127, 144:** Terra Muzick; **pp. 98, 146, 158, 176:** Anni Matsick; **pp. 92, 159–160, 162:** Pat Hoggan; **p. 102:** Mary O'Keefe Young; **pp. 107–109:** Evan Schwarze; **pp. 114, 213–214:** Three Communication Design; **p. 118:** Holly Graham; **pp. 124, 180:** Vera Rosenberry; **p. 128:** Cheryl Arnemann; **p. 132:** Betty Maxey; **p. 150:** Holly Jones; **p. 154:** Judith Sutton; **pp. 167–168:** Marika Hahn; **p. 172:** Sandra Shields; **pp. 185–186, 188–189:** Marlene Ekman; **pp. 209–210:** Paul Dolan

PHOTOGRAPHS

p. 120a, 120b: Jo Browne, Mick Smee/Tony Stone Worldwide; **p. 126b:** Uniphoto, Inc.; **pp. 126c, 167b:** Paul Barton/The Stock Market; **p. 126d:** Dan Bosler/Tony Stone Worldwide; **pp. 126e, 194c:** Ted Horowitz/The Stock Market; **p. 126f:** Into the Wind, Inc.; **p. 168:** Bill Bachman/Photo Edit; **p. 187b:** Paul Conklin/Photo Edit; **p. 187d:** Myrleen Ferguson Cate/Photo Edit; **p. 187e:** Mark Richards/Photo Edit; **p. 187f:** Don & Pat Valenti; **p. 193b:** Bruce Ayres/Tony Stone Worldwide; **p. 194a:** Bryan F. Peterson/The Stock Market; **p. 194b:** Gary Landsman/Uniphoto, Inc.; **p. 205:** AP/Wide World Photos

Unless otherwise acknowledged all photographs are the property of Addison-Wesley Educational Publishers Inc.

UNIT 1

CONTENTS

UNIT 2

UNIT 3

CONTENTS

UNIT 4

UNIT 5

CONTENTS

UNIT 6

BONUS PAGES

SPELLING DICTIONARY

THE WORD PLACE

Handwriting Models

PUNCH-OUTS

Big

Now I can catch and throw a ball
And spell
Cat. Dog.
And Pig.
I have finished being small
And started
Being Big.

Dorothy Aldis

Direction Words

1. Trace the **line**.

Draw a line.

2. This is a **picture**.

Underline the picture.

3. Trace the **circle**.

Draw a circle.

4. This is a **letter**.

Circle the letter.

c

c

5. This is a **word**.

Circle the word.

c a t

c a t

Ask your child to underline or to circle pictures and letters on a magazine page as you name them.

11

Direction Words

first   last

1. Color the **first** cat.

2. Color the **last** dog.

3. Underline the **first** letter.

c   a   t

4. Underline the **last** letter.

c   a   t

5. Underline the **first** word.

c a t   c a t   c a t

Direction Words

beginning   middle   ending

Circle the **beginning** letter in each word.

1. c a t

2. t o p

Circle the **middle** letter in each word.

3. b u s

4. t e n

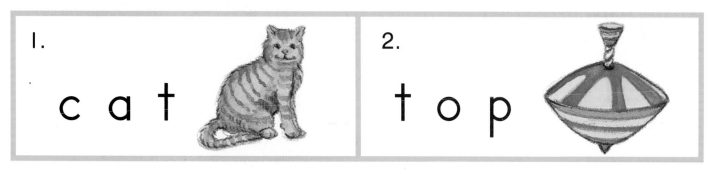

Circle the **ending** letter in each word.

5. b e d

6. p i n

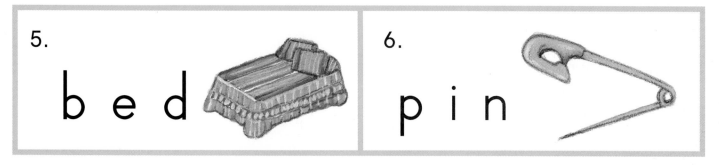

Write a list of three-letter words. Have your child point to the beginning, middle, or ending letter in each word.

Trace and Write

1. Trace the beginning letter.

2. Trace the middle letter.

3. Trace the ending letter.

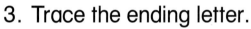

4. Trace the word **cat**.

5. Can you write the word **cat**?

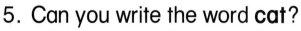

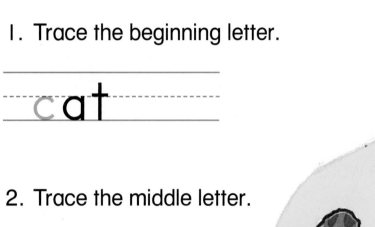

Letter Match

Look at the first letter.
Circle the letters that are the same.

1. c	a	c	o	c	e
2. B	B	R	B	P	D
3. g	g	d	g	p	g
4. M	M	W	N	M	Z
5. h	k	h	h	b	h
6. T	Y	T	I	F	T

Word Match

Look at the first word.
Circle the word that is the same.

1. up	pup	us	up
2. on	in	on	no
3. man	man	ran	men
4. top	pot	hot	top
5. kite	kite	like	kit
6. feed	need	feed	feel

Beginning Mm

Circle all the pictures that begin like  .

1.

2.

3.

Trace and write the letters.  moon

m m

M M

Beginning Gg

Circle all the pictures that begin like .

Trace and write the letters. **g**irl

Beginning Bb

Underline all the pictures that begin like  .

1.

2.

3.

Trace and write the letters.  **b**ook

b b

B B

Write **m, g,** and **b** on separate cards. Say words beginning with **m, g,** or **b,** and ask your child to hold up the card that shows how the word begins.

Beginning m, g, b

Listen to the beginning sound.
Write the beginning letter.

1. b

2. _____

3. _____

4. _____

5. _____

6. _____

7. _____

8. _____

9. _____

Beginning Ff

Circle all the pictures that begin like  .

1.

2.

3.

Trace and write the letters.  **f**ish

f f

F F

With your child, make up a tongue twister using words that begin like *fish*. *(Fay Fox forgot to feed five fish.)* Write the tongue twister, and have your child circle the **f**'s. Do the same using words that begin like *cat*.

Beginning Cc

Color all the pictures that begin like  .

1.

2.

3.

Trace and write the letters.  cat

c   c

C   C

Beginning Rr

Underline all the pictures that begin like  .

1.

2.

3.

Trace and write the letters.  **r**abbit

r r

R R

Have your child hop like a <u>rabbit</u> for each word you say beginning with **r,** swim like a <u>fish</u> for words beginning with **f,** or purr like a <u>cat</u> for words beginning with **c.**

23

Beginning f, c, r

Listen to the beginning sound.
Write the beginning letter.

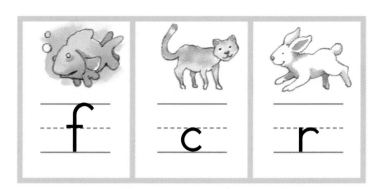

1.

2.

3.

4.

5.

6.

7.

8.

9.

Beginning Nn

Circle all the pictures that begin like  .

1.

2.

3.

Trace and write the letters.  **n**est

n n

N N

Can your child name more words that begin like *nest* or like *tent*? List the words as they are named.

25

Beginning Tt

Circle all the pictures that begin like  .

1.

2.

3.

Trace and write the letters.  tent

Beginning Ll

Underline all the pictures that begin like  .

1.

2.

3.

Trace and write the letters.  lion

Ask your child to draw two things that begin like *lion,* two that begin like *nest,* and two that begin like *tent.* Cut apart the pictures, and have your child match the pairs that begin with the same sound.

3

Beginning n, t, l

Listen to the beginning sound.
Write the beginning letter.

n   t   l

1.

2.

3.

4.

5.

6.

7.

8.

9.

Beginning Dd

Circle all the pictures that begin like  .

Trace and write the letters. **d**og

d   d

D   D

With your child, take turns naming other words that begin like *dog*. Do the same with words that begin like *valentine*.

29

Beginning Vv

Color all the pictures that begin like  .

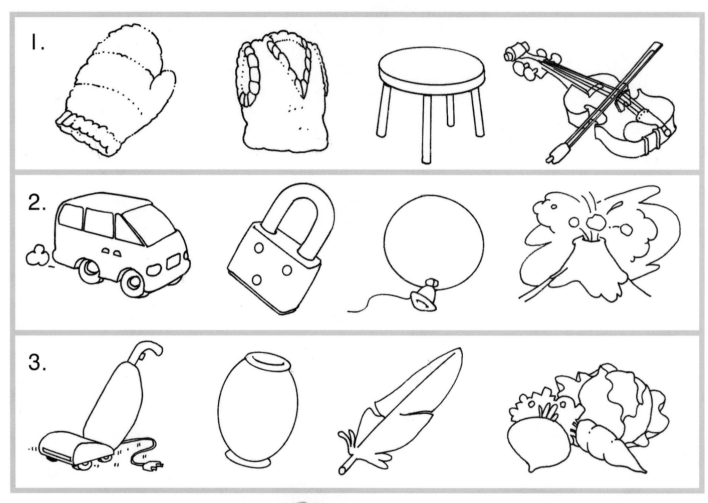

Trace and write the letters.  **v**alentine

V V

V V

Beginning Hh

Underline all the pictures that begin like  .

1.

2.

3.

Trace and write the letters.  **h**at

h h

H H

With your child, make up a tongue twister using words that begin like *hat*. (*Harry Hippo hates having haircuts*.) Write the sentence, and have your child circle the **h**'s. Do two other tongue twisters using words that begin like *dog* and like *valentine*.

31

Beginning d, v, h

Listen to the beginning sound.
Write the beginning letter.

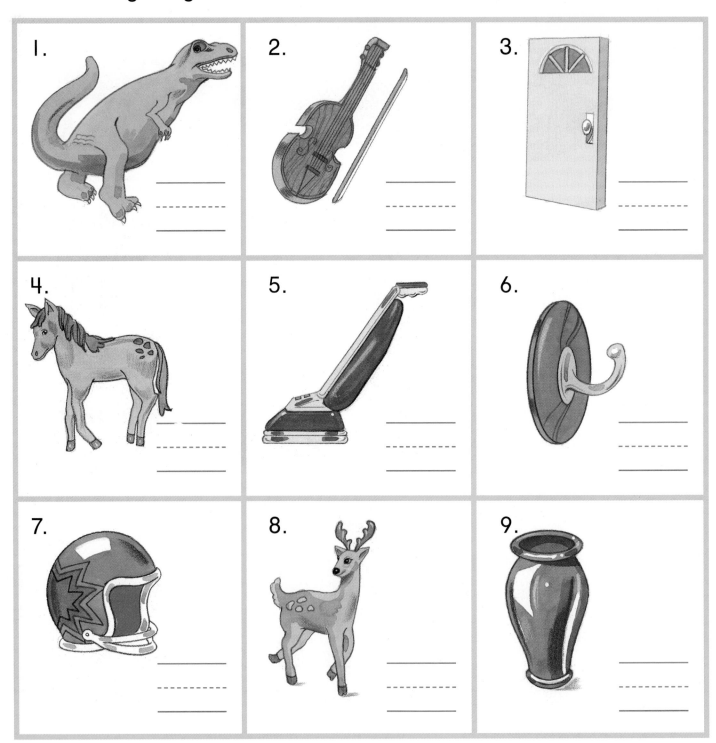

1.

2.

3.

4.

5.

6.

7.

8.

9.

Beginning Ss

Circle all the pictures that begin like  .

1.

2.

3.

Trace and write the letters.  **s**un

S S

S S

Beginning Pp

Underline all the pictures that begin like  .

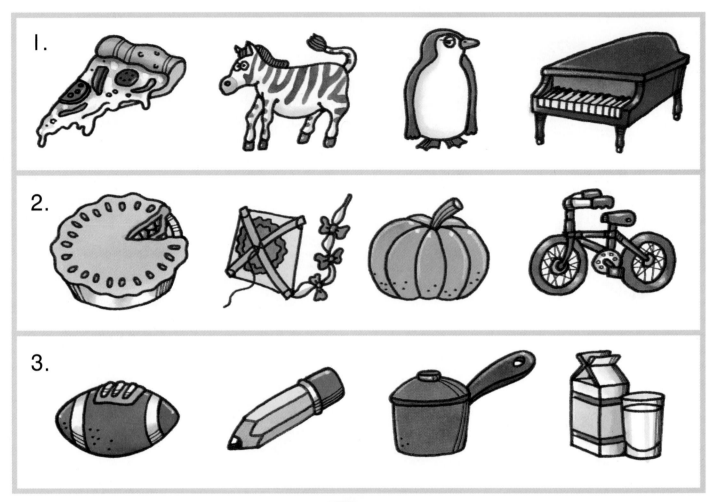

1.

2.

3.

Trace and write the letters.  **p**ig

p   p
P   P

Beginning Yy

Circle all the pictures that begin like  .

Trace and write the letters.  yarn

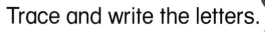

Y Y

Y Y

 Ask your child to draw something silly that begins with **s**, something pink that begins with **p**, and something yellow that begins with **y**.

Beginning s, p, y

Listen to the beginning sound.
Write the beginning letter.

s   p   y

1. _____

2. _____

3. _____

4. _____

5. _____

6. _____

7. _____

8. _____

9. _____

Beginning Zz

Circle all the pictures that begin like .

1.

2.

3.

Trace and write the letters.  **zebra**

z z

Z Z

Beginning Jj

Color all the pictures that begin like  .

1.

2.

3.

Trace and write the letters.  jeep

j   j

J   J

Beginning Kk

Underline all the pictures that begin like  .

1.

2.

3.

Trace and write the letters.  **k**ey

k k

K K

Have your child do a karate kick for each word you say beginning with **k** *(kid, kind, kiss, keep)* and wiggle for each word you say beginning with **w** *(water, wash, will, wag).*

39

Beginning Ww

Circle all the pictures that begin like  .

Trace and write the letters.  **w**eb

W W

W W

Writing Qq and Xx

queen

Trace and write the letters.

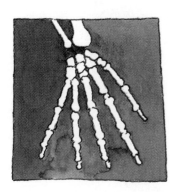

X ray

Trace and write the letters.

 To review **z, j, k,** and **w** (see p. 42), have your child draw a zoo with animals whose names begin with those letters: *zebra, jaguar, koala,* and *walrus.*

41

Beginning z, j, k, w

Listen to the beginning sound.
Write the beginning letter.

z   j   k   w

1.

2.

3.

4.

5.

6.

7.

8.

9.

Ending n, s

5

Circle all the pictures that end like  train .

1.

2.

Circle all the pictures that end like  bus .

3.

4.

 Write **n, s, d,** and **p** on separate cards. Say words ending with those letters *(bacon, twin; plus, toss; cold, head; hoop, trip)*. Ask your child to hold up the card that shows how the word <u>ends</u>.

Ending d, p

Underline all the pictures that end like  bed .

1.

2.

Underline all the pictures that end like cap .

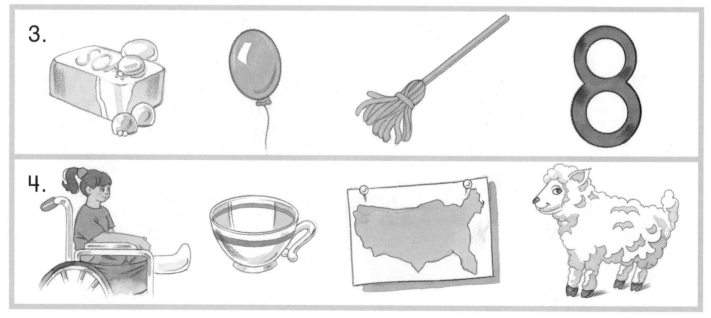

3.

4.

Ending t, g

Color all the pictures that end like  goat .

Color all the pictures that end like  bug .

Ending n, s, d, p, t, g

Listen to the ending sound.
Write the ending letter.

n	s	d
p	t	g

1.

2.

3.

4.

5.

6.

7.

8.

9.

Ending m, k

Circle all the pictures that end like jam .

Circle all the pictures that end like  hoo**k**.

Write these word parts in a list: *ja–, hoo–, ha–, ca–, we–*. Have your child write **m, k, r,** or **b** to finish each word. More than one answer is possible.

Ending r, b

Underline all the pictures that end like star .

Underline all the pictures that end like  crib .

Ending f, l, x

Color all the pictures that end like leaf .

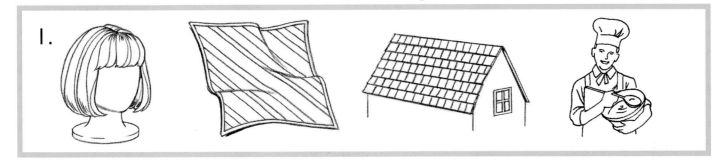

1.

Color all the pictures that end like  pool .

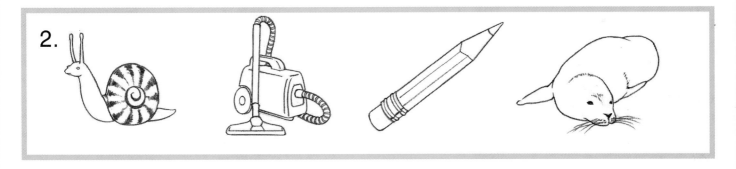

2.

Color all the pictures that end like  fox .

3.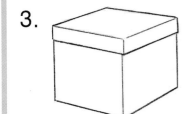

5

Ending m, k, r, b, f, l, x

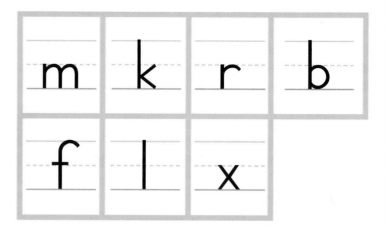

Listen to the ending sound.
Write the ending letter.

1.

2.

3.

4.

5.

6.

7.

8.

9.

Short a: Rhyme

Circle all the pictures that rhyme with .

Circle all the pictures that rhyme with .

 How many words can your child think of that rhyme with the following words: *bat, man, sack, cab, mad, lap?* Write a list for each set of rhyming words.

51

Short a: Word Families

Say the names of the pictures.
Write **at** to make each word.

b a t

1. m _____

2. c _____

3. h _____

Say the names of the pictures.
Write **an** to make each word.

m a n

4. v _____

5. p _____

6. c _____

Short e: Rhyme

Circle all the pictures that rhyme with  .

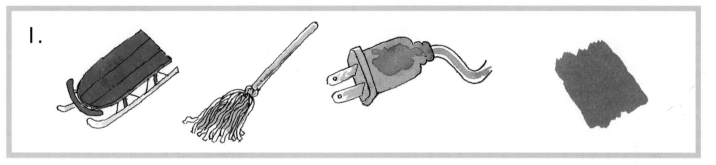

1.

Circle all the pictures that rhyme with  .

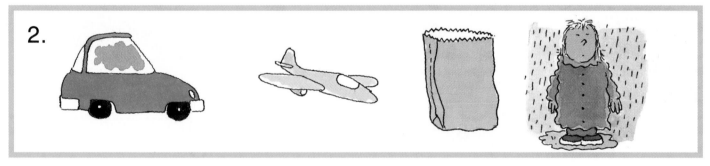

2.

Circle all the pictures that rhyme with  .

3.

Short e: Word Families

Say the names of the pictures.
Write **ed** to make each word.

b ed

1. r

2. s l

Say the names of the pictures.
Write **et** to make each word.

n et

3. W

4. j

Say the names of the pictures.
Write **en** to make each word.

p en

5. h

6. t

Short i: Rhyme

Circle all the pictures that rhyme with  .

1.

Circle all the pictures that rhyme with  .

2.

Circle all the pictures that rhyme with 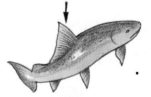 .

3.

Have your child name one word that rhymes with each of these names: *Jim, Chris, Jill, Nick, Lin*. Write the rhyming word pairs.

Short i: Word Families

Say the names of the pictures.
Write **it** to make each word.

h<u>it</u>

1. s _____

2. k _____

Say the names of the pictures.
Write **ig** to make each word.

d<u>ig</u>

3. b _____

4. p _____

Say the names of the pictures.
Write **in** to make each word.

f<u>in</u>

5. w _____

6. p _____

Short o: Rhyme

Circle all the pictures that rhyme with  .

Circle all the pictures that rhyme with  .

Short o: Word Families

Say the names of the pictures.
Write **op** to make each word.

top

1. h

2. sh

3. m

Say the names of the pictures.
Write **ot** to make each word.

hot

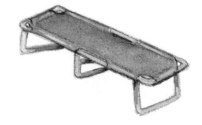

4. p

5. c

6. sp

Short u: Rhyme

Circle all the pictures that rhyme with  .

1.

Circle all the pictures that rhyme with  .

2.

Circle all the pictures that rhyme with  .

3.

How many words can your child think of that rhyme with the following words: *sun, bug, drum, jump, cut*? Write a list for each set of rhyming words.

59
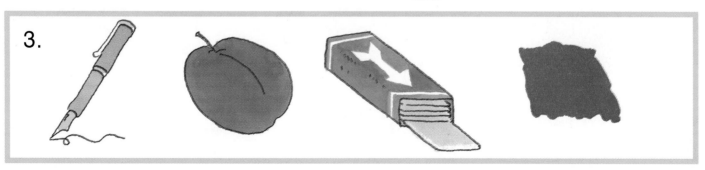

Short u: Word Families

Say the names of the pictures.
Write **un** to make each word.

s un

1. f

2. r

Say the names of the pictures.
Write **ug** to make each word.

b ug

3. h

4. r

Say the names of the pictures.
Write **um** to make each word.

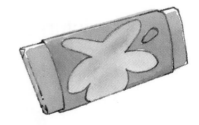

d rum

5. pl

6. g

Name

About Me

Writer's Word Bank

about
again
all
always
and
are
as
away

be
because
birthday
but
by

came
come
could

do
does
down

eat
end
every
everybody

favorite
find
first
for
friend
from

get
girl
give
go
going
good

has
have
her
here
him
his
home
house
how

I
into
is

like
little
live
look
love

make
many
more
my

new
nice
not
now

of
on
once
one
or
other
our
out
outside
over

part
party
people
play
pretty
put

said
saw
school
see
so
some

thank
that
the
their
them
then
there
these
they
to
too
two

under
use

very

want
was
we
went
were
what
when
where
who
will
with
would

you
your

How to Study a Word

Here are five steps to help you learn to spell.

1. **Look** at the word.

2. **Say** the word.

3. **Listen** to the sounds.

4. **Write** the word.

5. **Check** the spelling.

Words with Short a

Look at each word. Say it.
Listen for the short a sound in .
Write each word. Check it.

at	1. at
bat	2. bat
cat	3. cat
an	4. an
man	5. man
ran	6. ran

Everyday Words

Write each word.

and	7. and
am	8. am

Print the letters **a, t, n, b, c, m,** and **r** on separate pieces of paper. Ask your child to spell each list word using these letters.

at	an
bat	man
cat	ran

Write the list words that rhyme with ⟶.

1. an   2. _____   3. _____

Write the list words that rhyme with ⟶.

4. at   5. _____   6. _____

Write the missing list words.

7. The dog has the b_____ .

8. The c_____ has the ball.

| and | am |

Write the missing letters.
Then write the words.

9. __ m   _____

10. __ __ d   _____

7

at	an
bat	man
cat	ran

Name the pictures.
Write the missing letters.

1. ___ a ___

2. ___ a ___

3. ___ a ___

Finish the sentence.
Use a list word.

4. I see

Write a sentence.
Use the word **and** or **am** .

5. _____

Write two words that tell about animals.

MY WORDS

Help your child practice for a spelling test. Say each word, use it in a sentence, repeat the word, and have your child write it.

67

at	an
bat	man
cat	ran

Read about a trip to a farm.
Write the missing list words.

1. We had fun _____ the farm.

2. A dog _____ to meet us.

3. A _____ showed us the animals.

4. We saw a _____ fly out of the barn.

5. A _____ ran after a mouse.

6. A hen laid _____ egg.

Words with Short e

Look at each word. Say it.
Listen for the short e sound in .
Write each word. Check it.

bed	1. bed
led	2. led
met	3. met
get	4. get
pen	5. pen
ten	6. ten

Write each word.

yes	7. yes
then	8. then

Spell each list word aloud and ask your child to say the word. Then say each word and ask your child to spell it.

8

bed	get
led	pen
met	ten

Write the list words that rhyme with **pet**.

1. m _____   2. g _____

Write the list words that rhyme with **red**.

3. b _____   4. l _____

Write the list words that rhyme with **hen**.

5. p _____   6. t _____

How many hens are in the pen?

7. _____

| yes | then |

Write a word in each shape.
Then write the word.

8. _____

9. _____

bed	get
led	pen
met	ten

Name the pictures.
Write the missing letters.

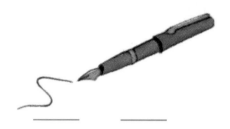

1. __ e __

2. __ e __

3. __ e __

Finish the sentence.
Use a list word.

4. We _____

Write a sentence.
Use the word **yes** or **then** .

5. _____

Think of two things you find in a zoo.
Write their names.

_____ _____

bed	get
led	pen
met	ten

Read about a zoo.

Write the missing list words.

1. We got out of _____ .

2. Let's _____ to the zoo!

3. A woman _____ us at the gate.

4. She _____ us to the lion house.

5. We saw _____ lions.

6. Lion cubs played in a big _____ .

Words with Short i

Look at each word. Say it.
Listen for the short i sound in  .
Write each word. Check it.

sit	1. sit
hit	2. hit
big	3. big
dig	4. dig
in	5. in
pin	6. pin

Write each word.

it	7. it
will	8. will

sit	dig
hit	in
big	pin

Write the list words that rhyme with **pig**.

1. d _____

2. b _____

Write the list words that rhyme with **win**.

3. i _____

4. p _____

Write the list words that rhyme with **fit**.

5. h _____

6. s _____

Write the missing list word.

7. This fish is _____ a bowl.

| it | will |

Read the sentences.
Write the missing words in the puzzle.

8. He ____ get a pet fish.

9. What will he name ____?

8.	9.		
	i		

sit	dig
hit	in
big	pin

Write the letter **i**.

1. i ___ ___ ___ ___ ___ ___ ___ ___ ___

Did you add a dot to each **i?**

Write **hit.**

2. h

Write **dig.**

3. d

Write **pin.**

4. p

What can a pet do in a pet show?
Finish the sentence. Use a list word.

5. A pet _____

Write a sentence.
Use **it** or **will** .

6. _____

Write two words that tell what pets can do.

MY WORDS _____   _____

sit	dig
hit	in
big	pin

Read about a pet show.
Write the missing list words.

1. Today is the _____ day.

2. Two cats _____ down.

3. Two dogs _____ up bones.

4. A hen is _____ a cage.

5. A man will _____ on the ribbons.

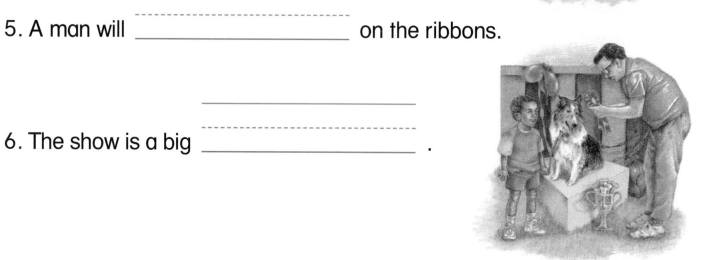

6. The show is a big _____ .

Words with Short o

Look at each word. **Say** it.
Listen for the **short o** sound in .
Write each word. **Check** it.

hop	1. hop
top	2. top
mop	3. mop
hot	4. hot
pot	5. pot
got	6. got

Everyday Words

Write each word.

on	7. on
box	8. box

hop	hot
top	pot
mop	got

Read the clues.
Write the list words.

It begins like ____ .

1. ____

It begins like ____ .

2. ____

It begins like ____ .

3. ____

It begins like ____ .

4. ____

Two words begin like ____ .

5. ____

6. ____

What does a rabbit do?
Write the list word.

7. ____

on	box

Write the words that begin
with these letters.
Then write the words.

8. b ____ ____

9. o ____ ____

hop	hot
top	pot
mop	got

Listen for the **ot** in **hot**.
Write **ot** to make new words.

1. d

2. n

3. l

Listen for the **op** in **top**.
Write **op** to make new words.

4. p

5. st

6. sh

Tell where a pet is hiding.
Finish the sentence. Use a list word.

7. The

Write a sentence.
Use the word **on** or **box** .

8.

Write two names for pets.

 MY WORDS

Write **ot** and **op** at the top of two columns. Ask your child to write three spelling words that end with **ot** and three that end with **op.**

79

hop	hot
top	pot
mop	got

Read about pets.

Write the missing list words.

1. Who _____ a new pet?

2. Is the _____ on the fish food?

3. Can the frog _____ out?

4. Is the dog too _____ ?

5. Who broke the _____ ?

6. Did you use the _____ ?

Number Words

How old are you?
Listen to the poem.
Think about how you have grown.

11

The End

When I was One,
I had just begun.

When I was Two,
I was nearly new.

When I was Three,
I was hardly Me.

When I was Four,
I was not much more.

When I was Five,
I was just alive.

But now I am Six, I'm as clever as clever.
So I think I'll be six now for ever and ever.

A. A. Milne

Read the poem aloud. Encourage your child to say and point to the number words as you read.

81

Look at each word. **Say** it.
Write each word. **Check** it.

one	1. one
two	2. two
three	3. three
four	4. four
five	5. five
six	6. six

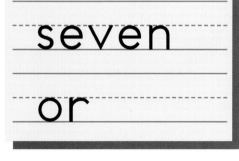

Everyday Words

Write each word.

seven	7. seven
or	8. or

one	four
two	five
three	six

Write the word that tells how many you see.

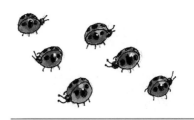

1. _____

2. _____

3. _____

4. _____

5. _____

6. _____

Finish the sentence about growing up.
Use a number word.

7. I am _____

seven	or

Write the missing words.

_____

8. Are you six _____ seven?

_____

9. Jill is _____ .

Choose groups of items, such as five beans or three pencils. Ask your child to say how many and then spell the number word.

83

11

one	four
two	five
three	six

Write the number words to finish the
jump rope rhyme.

1. _____ ,

2. _____ ,

Buckle my shoe.

3. _____ ,

4. _____ ,

Shut the door.

5. _____ ,

6. _____ ,

Pick up sticks.

Review

Lesson 7: Short a

Lesson 8: Short e

Lesson 9: Short i

Lesson 10: Short o

Lesson 11: Number Words

UNIT REVIEW LIST

at	bed	sit	hop	one
bat	led	hit	top	two
cat	met	big	mop	three
an	get	dig	hot	four
man	pen	in	pot	five
ran	ten	pin	got	six

Word Sort

Write the words that go in each list.

at	an
bat	man
cat	ran

Words with **-an**

1. _____

2. _____

3. _____

Words with **-at**

4. _____

5. _____

6. _____

ABC Order

Write these words in ABC order.

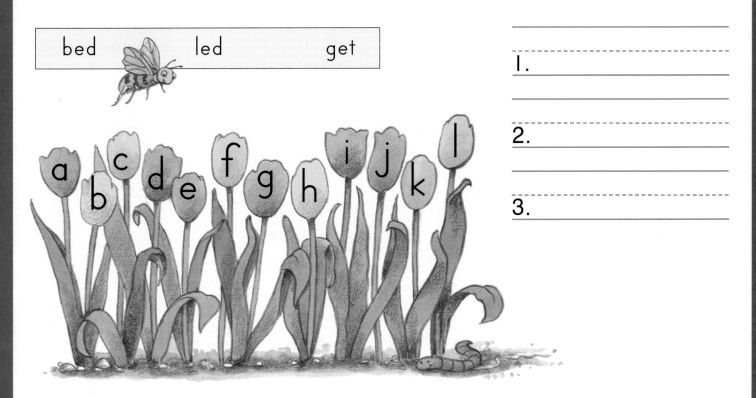

| bed | led | get |

1. _____

2. _____

3. _____

Now write these words in ABC order.

| pen | ten | met |

4. _____

5. _____

6. _____

Beginning Sounds

Write the list words that have the same beginning sound.

It begins like  .

_____

1. _____

It begins like  .

_____

2. _____

It begins like .

_____

3. _____

It begins like  .

_____

4. _____

It begins like .

_____

5. _____

It begins like it .

_____

6. _____

Ending Sounds

Write the list words that have the same ending sounds.

hop	hot
top	pot
mop	got

Words that end like

_____   _____   _____

1. _____   2. _____   3. _____

Words that end like

_____   _____   _____

4. _____   5. _____   6. _____

Crossword Puzzles

Write the list word for each answer.

one	four
two	five
three	six

1. Rhymes with

2. Rhymes with

3. Rhymes with

4. Rhymes with

5. Rhymes with **mix**

6. Rhymes with **dive**

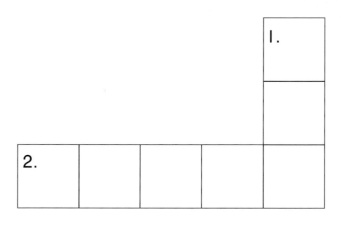

My Favorite Story

Words with Short u

Look at each word. Say it.
Listen for the short u sound in  .
Write each word. Check it.

13

fun	1.
sun	2.
us	3.
bus	4.
up	5.
cup	6.

Everyday Words

Write each word.

but	7.
cut	8.

Say sentences such as "We'll have fun in the sun," "The bus stopped for us," and "Pick up the cup." Ask your child to repeat the words that rhyme and then spell them.

fun	bus
sun	up
us	cup

Write the **short u** words with three letters.

1. _____ 2. _____

3. _____ 4. _____

Write the **short u** words with two letters.

5. _____ 6. _____

Write the missing list words.

7. Here comes the _____ .

8. It's coming for _____ !

but	cut

Write a word in each shape.
Then write the word.

9. _____

10. _____

fun	bus
sun	up
us	cup

These words sound the same.
They have different meanings and spellings.

son    **sun**

a boy child   gives heat and light

Write the word that makes sense.

1. A boy is a father's _____ .

2. The _____ will set at 7:00.

How does your family have fun?
Write a sentence. Use a list word.

3. _____

Write a sentence.
Use the word **but** or **cut**.

4. _____

Write two words you think are fun.

MY WORDS ▶   _____   _____

Help your child practice for a spelling test. Say each word, use it in a sentence, repeat the word, and have your child write it.

93

fun	bus
sun	up
us	cup

Read the invitation to a picnic.
Write the missing list words.

1. Please come with _____ .

2. You'll have _____ .

3. We'll pick you _____ .

4. Then we'll get on the _____ .

5. The _____ will shine.

6. Bring a paper _____ .

Words with Long a

Look at each word. **Say** it.
Listen for the **long a** sound in  .
Write each word. **Check** it.

made

came

gave

late

say

day

1. _____   _____

2. _____   _____

3. _____   _____

4. _____   _____

5. _____   _____

6. _____   _____

Everyday Words

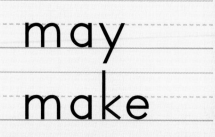

Write each word.

may

make

7. _____   _____

8. _____   _____

Read the clues. Write the list words.

made	late
came	say
gave	day

It rhymes with .

_____

1. _____

It rhymes with .

_____

2. _____

It rhymes with .

_____

3. _____

It rhymes with .

_____

4. _____

Two words rhyme with .

_____

5. _____

_____

6. _____

Write the missing list words.

7. Mom _____ home at 6:00.

8. She _____ me a hug.

| may | make |

Read the sentences. Write the missing words in the puzzle.

9. Can you ____ up a game?

10. You ____ go home now.

made	late
came	say
gave	day

A sentence is a group of words that tells about someone or something.

Write each group of words that is a sentence.

1. Alex.   Alex made lunch.

2. The bus came late.   Came late.

Write a sentence about a good day.
Use a list word.

3.

Write a sentence.
Use the word **may** or **make**.

4.

Write two words for something you can make.

 MY WORDS ▶

Say a clue for each spelling word, such as, "This word means the opposite of *early*." Ask your child to write the spelling word that fits your clue.

97

made	late
came	say
gave	day

Read about Grandma's visit.
Write the missing list words.

1. Grandma _____ to our house.

2. We _____ a cake together.

3. We _____ some to our friends.

4. We had fun all _____ .

5. Now it is _____ .

6. We'll _____ good-by to Grandma.

Words with Long e

Look at each word. **Say** it.
Listen for the **long e** sound in  .
Write each word. **Check** it.

we
she
me
he
tree
feed

1.

2.

3.

4.

5.

6.

Everyday Words

Write each word.

see
a

7.

8.

Say each spelling word and ask your child if the **long e** sound is spelled with one e or two. Then have your child spell the word.

we	he
she	tree
me	feed

Use this secret code.
Write the list words.

w e m h s d t r f

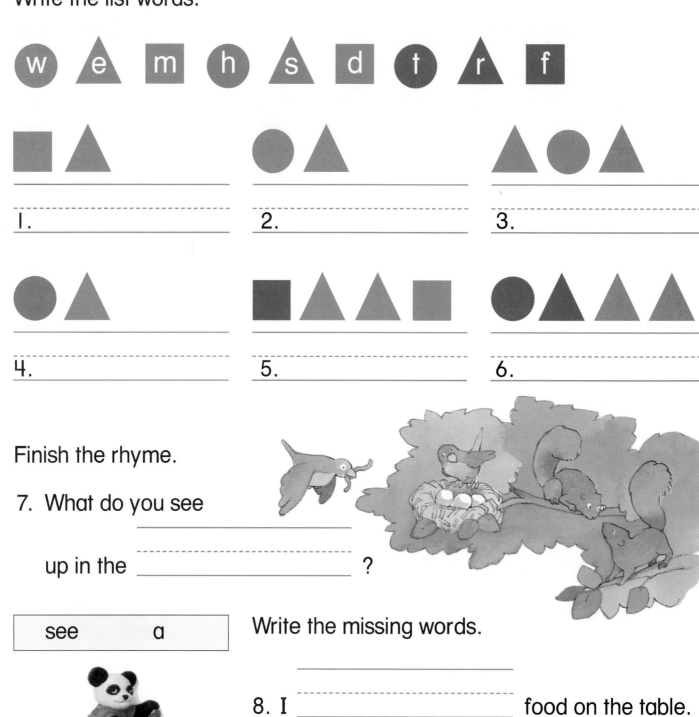

1. _____

2. _____

3. _____

4. _____

5. _____

6. _____

Finish the rhyme.

7. What do you see

_____

up in the _____ ?

see	a

Write the missing words.

8. I _____ food on the table.

9. Do you want _____ sandwich?

we	he
she	tree
me	feed

Read each sentence.

Write the list words that can take the place

of the underlined words.

1. First, <u>Sarah</u> will make lunch.

_____

- -

_____

2. Next, <u>Mom and I</u> will feed the baby.

_____

- -

_____

Write a sentence about lunch.

Use a list word.

_____

3. _____

Write a sentence.

Use the word **see** or **a**.

_____

4. _____

Write two words for things you eat for lunch.

MY WORDS ▶   _____   _____

- - - - - - - - - - - - - - -   - - - - - - - - - - - - -

we	he
she	tree
me	feed

Read about helping with lunch.
Write the missing list words.

1. Let's eat under this _____ .

2. When can _____ all eat?

3. Grandma needs help.

Today _____ asks us to help.

4. Who will help _____
make lunch?

5. Dad will _____ the baby now.

6. Then _____ will sit with us.

Words with Long i

Look at each word. Say it.
Listen for the long i sound in  .
Write each word. Check it.

like

nice

time

ride

my

cry

1. _____

2. _____

3. _____

4. _____

5. _____

6. _____

Write each word.

by

bike

7. _____

8. _____

Cover the bottom of a small pan with sand or salt. Have your child use a finger to write each word in the sand or salt.

103

Write the missing list word below each sentence.

like	ride
nice	my
time	cry

1. What ____ is it?

_____

2. This is ____ book.

_____

3. Don't ____.

_____

4. I ____ you.

_____

5. Mice are ____ .

_____

6. He can ____ .

_____

by	bike

Write the missing words.

_____

7. I'll ride my _____
   to Grandpa's house.

_____

8. Grandpa's house is _____
   the lake.

like	ride
nice	my
time	cry

A telling sentence begins with a capital letter.
It ends with a period.

Write each sentence.
Begin with a capital letter. End with a period.

1. it is time to go

_____

2. i will ride my bike

_____

Write a sentence. Tell how you help.
Use a list word.

3. _____

Write a sentence.
Use the word **by** or **bike** .

4. _____

Write two words you want to learn to spell.

MY WORDS _____   _____

like	ride
nice	my
time	cry

Read about how Dan helps Kim.
Write the missing list words.

1. Kim wants to _____ her new bike.

2. Her brother Dan is _____ .

3. Dan says, "I will help _____ sister."

4. Kim falls off her bike one _____ .

5. She starts to _____ .

6. She would _____ a hug.

Name

Color Words

Listen to the poem.
What colors do you see around you?

Yellow

Green is go,
and red is stop,
and yellow is peaches
with cream on top.

Earth is brown,
and blue is sky;
yellow looks well
on a butterfly.

Clouds are white,
black, pink, or
mocha;
yellow's a dish of
tapioca.

David McCord

Look at each word. **Say** it.
Listen to its sounds.
Write each word. **Check** it.

red
green
blue
yellow
brown
black

1. _____

2. _____

3. _____

4. _____

5. _____

6. _____

Write each word.

for
to

7. _____

8. _____

Name

red	yellow
green	brown
blue	black

The things in each picture are the same color.
Write the word that names the color.

1. _____

2. _____

3. _____

4. _____

5. _____

6. _____

Write a sentence about your favorite color.

7. _____

| for | to |

Write the missing letters. Then write the words.

8. f __ r _____

9. t __ _____

red	yellow
green	brown
blue	black

Look at the picture.
Write the missing color words.

1. Mom's cap is _____ .

2. Dad's shirt is _____ .

3. The girl has a _____ ball.

4. The boy has a _____ pail.

5. Their dog has _____ spots.

6. The basket is _____ .

Review

Lesson 13: Short u

Lesson 14: Long a

Lesson 15: Long e

Lesson 16: Long i

Lesson 17: Color Words

UNIT REVIEW LIST

fun	made	we	like	red
sun	came	she	nice	green
us	gave	me	time	blue
bus	late	he	ride	yellow
up	say	tree	my	brown
cup	day	feed	cry	black

Ending Sounds

Write the list words that have the same ending sounds.

fun	bus
sun	up
us	cup

Words that end like
circus

1. _____

2. _____

Words that end like
pup

3. _____

4. _____

Words that end like
run

5. _____

6. _____

ABC Order

Write these words in ABC order.

day	gave	came

1. _____

2. _____

3. _____

Now write these words in ABC order.

late	say	made

4. _____

5. _____

6. _____

Word Search

Find the words. Circle the words.
Write the words you found.

we	he
she	tree
me	feed

```
w  e  x  b  h  e  v
c  t  r  e  e  k  n
l  p  f  e  e  d  z
s  h  e  u  m  e  o
```

1. _____

2. _____

3. _____

4. _____

5. _____

6. _____

Rhyming Words

Write the list word that
rhymes with each word.

like	ride
nice	my
time	cry

It rhymes with **slide.**

1. _____

It rhymes with **bike.**

2. _____

It rhymes with **dime.**

3. _____

It rhymes with **mice.**

4. _____

Two words rhyme with **by.**

5. _____

6. _____

Crossword Puzzles

Write the color words in the puzzles.

1.

2.

3.

4.

5.

6.

A Special Trip

Words with Long o

Look at each word. **Say** it.
Listen for the **long o** sound in .
Write each word. **Check** it.

no	1.
so	2.
rode	3.
nose	4.
stone	5.
hope	6.

Everyday Words

Write each word.

those	7.
never	8.

Write the letters **n, r, h, st, s,** and **n** in a column. Say each spelling word and ask your child to finish writing the word after its beginning letter(s).

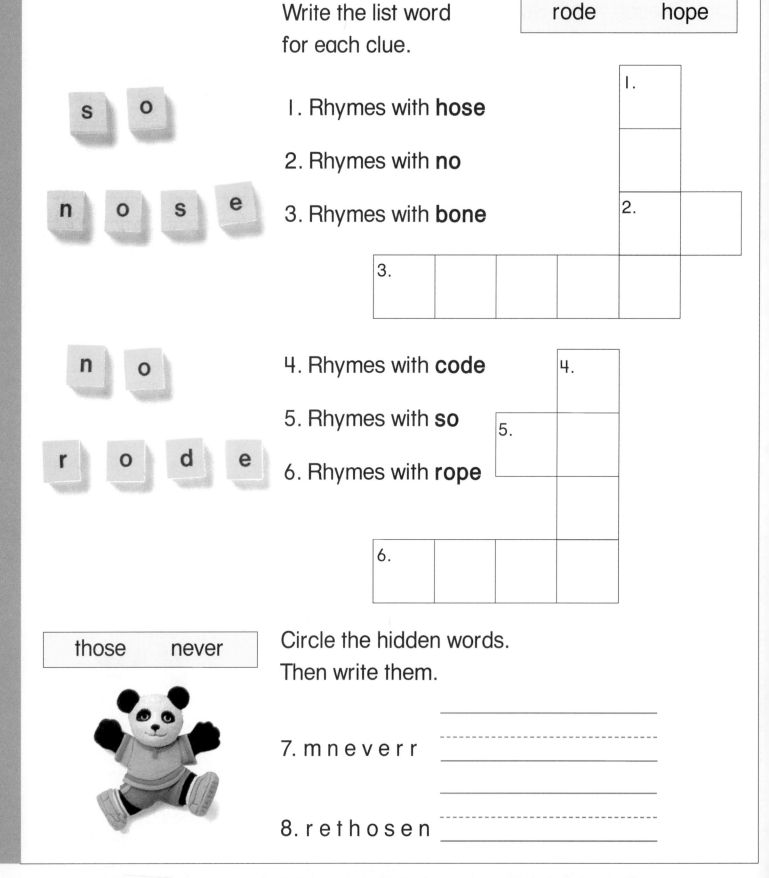

no	nose
so	stone
rode	hope

Write the list word
for each clue.

1. Rhymes with **hose**

2. Rhymes with **no**

3. Rhymes with **bone**

4. Rhymes with **code**

5. Rhymes with **so**

6. Rhymes with **rope**

those	never

Circle the hidden words.
Then write them.

7. m n e v e r r _____

_____

8. r e t h o s e n _____

no	nose
so	stone
rode	hope

Circle each list word that is spelled wrong.
Then write the sentences correctly.

1. We hop to see you soon.

_____

- -

_____

2. He rod his bike.

_____

- -

_____

3. She found a small ston.

_____

- -

_____

What would you write in a letter?
Write a sentence. Use a list word.

- -

4. _____

Write a sentence.
Use the word **those** or **never** .

- -

5. _____

Write two words you would use in a letter.

- - - - - - - -   - - - - - - - -

_____   _____

Read Ray's letter from summer camp.
Write the missing list words.

no	nose
so	stone
rode	hope

Dear Mom and Dad,

_____

1. We _____ on horses.

_____

2. I climbed over a _____ wall.

_____

3. I am having _____ much fun!

_____

4. My _____ is red from the sun.

_____

5. There are _____ bugs!

_____

6. I _____ I can come back.

Love,
Ray

Words with Final e

Look at each word. **Say** it.
Listen to its sounds.
Write each word. **Check** it.

tap	1.	
tape	2.	
rip	3.	
ripe	4.	
not	5.	
note	6.	

Write each word.

as	7.	
ate	8.	

Print the letters **t, a, p, e, r, i, n,** and **o** on separate pieces of paper. Ask your child to spell each list word using these letters.

tap	ripe
tape	not
rip	note

Write the words that go in each list.
Then circle the words with final **e.**

Words with a **long vowel** sound

1. _____ 2. _____ 3. _____

Words with a **short vowel** sound

4. _____ 5. _____ 6. _____

Write the missing list words.

7. Please write me a _____ today.

8. Do _____ put it off!

as	ate

Write the missing words.

9. He is as tall _____ I am.

10. She _____ all of the apples.

Name

tap	ripe
tape	not
rip	note

Write each asking sentence.
Begin with a capital letter.
End with a question mark **?** .

1. are the apples ripe

_____

- -

_____

2. who will read the note

_____

- -

_____

3. do you have the tape

_____

- -

_____

Write a sentence about a garden.
Use a list word.

_____

- -
4.

Write a sentence. Use the word **as** or **ate** .

_____

- -
5.

Write the names of two things in a garden.

MY WORDS ▶   _____   _____

- - - - - - - - - -   - - - - - - - - - -

_____   _____

The berries are not ready.
How can the children let everyone know?
Write the missing list words.

tap	ripe
tape	not
rip	note

1. There is a _____ in the paper.

2. Fix it with _____ .

3. Now write a _____ .

4. Please do _____ pick the berries.

5. They are not _____ .

6. Hold up the note.

I will _____ in the nails.

Adding -s

Sometimes you add **-s** to name more than one.

Look at each word. **Say** it.

Does it have **-s** added?

Write each word. **Check** it.

friend

friends

game

games

kite

kites

1. _____

2. _____

3. _____

4. _____

5. _____

6. _____

Everyday Words

Write each word.

teacher

some

7. _____

8. _____

Say the word *friend*, use it in a sentence, and ask your child to spell it. Then ask your child to say the word for more than one friend, use it in a sentence, and spell it. Repeat for *game* and *kite*.

Write the missing list word below each picture.

friend	games
friends	kite
game	kites

1. playing ____

2. good ____

3. a baseball ____

4. flying ____

5. my best ____

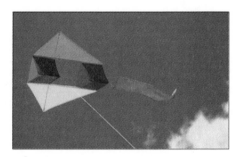

6. a big ____

teacher   some

Write the words that begin with these letters.
Then write the words.

7. S ____ _____

8. t ____ _____

Name ....

friend	games
friends	kite
game	kites

An **-s** makes a naming word mean more than one.

one kite   two kites

Write the naming words that mean more than one.

1. one bed   two _____

2. one cat   three _____

3. one cup   four _____

4. one stone   five _____

Write a sentence about a friend.
Use a list word.

5. _____

Write a sentence.
Use the word **teacher** or **some.**

6. _____

Write two words for things you do with friends.

   _____   _____

Say a clue for each spelling word, such as, "This word means *pal.*" Ask your child to write the spelling word that fits
your clue.

127

friend   games
friends   kite
game   kites

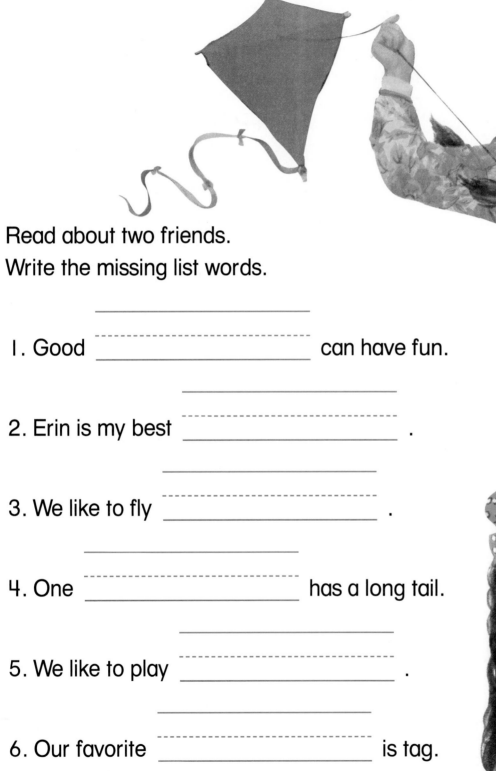

Read about two friends.
Write the missing list words.

1. Good _____ can have fun.

2. Erin is my best _____ .

3. We like to fly _____ .

4. One _____ has a long tail.

5. We like to play _____ .

6. Our favorite _____ is tag.

Words to Know

Look at each word. **Say** it.
Write each word. **Check** it.

is

are

was

were

has

had

1. _____

2. _____

3. _____

4. _____

5. _____

6. _____

Everyday Words

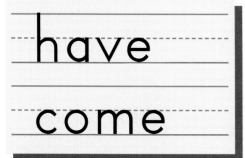

Write each word.

have

come

7. _____

8. _____

A shape and color stand for each letter.
Use this secret code to write the list words.

is	were
are	has
was	had

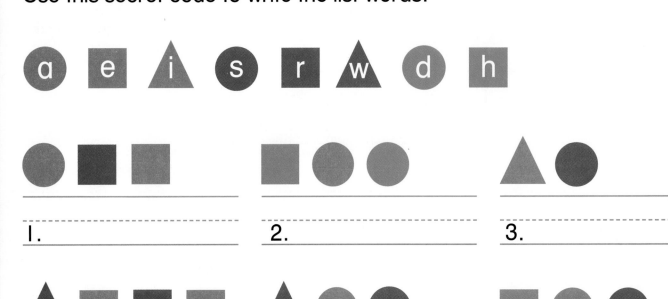

a e i s r w d h

1. _____

2. _____

3. _____

4. _____

5. _____

6. _____

Write the missing letters.

7. ___ ___ d

8. i ___ ___

9. w ___ r ___

have	come

Write the missing words.

10. They will _____ to see us.

11. We _____ some games.

is	were
are	has
was	had

Some words are made from two words.
An apostrophe ' takes the place of
missing letters.

He is here.   **He's** here.

Write the two underlined words as one word.

<u>She is</u> happy.

1. _____

<u>He is</u> my friend.

2. _____

<u>He is</u> six.

3. _____

<u>She is</u> nice.

4. _____

<u>She is</u> big.

5. _____

<u>He is</u> late.

6. _____

Write a sentence about a party.
Use a list word.

7. _____

Write a sentence.
Use the word **have** or **come** .

8. _____

Write the names of two things you find at parties.

MY WORDS

_____   _____

Write each spelling word on an index card. Say the word as you show a card. Hold the card behind you and ask your child to spell the word.

131

Read about John's birthday.
Write the missing list words.

is	were
are	has
was	had

1. Yesterday _____ John's
   birthday.

2. We _____ a birthday party
   for him.

3. Five friends _____ there.

4. Now John _____ new skates.

5. He _____ very happy.

6. Today, we _____ going to
   the park to skate.

Animal Words

Listen to the poem.

Think about a pet you would like to have.

What would your pet look like?

I Would Like to Have a Pet

I would like to have a pet,
any kind at all.
Something big,
something small,
something sleeping in the hall
would be just fine.
I would like to have a pet.
Will you be mine?

Karla Kuskin

Read the poem aloud. Ask your child to find and say the word *pet* as you reread the poem.
You may want to talk with your child about the different kinds of animals that make good pets.

Look at each word. Say it.
Listen to its sounds.
Write each word. Check it.

kitten

frog

dog

fish

puppy

pet

1. _____   _____

2. _____   _____

3. _____   _____

4. _____   _____

5. _____   _____

6. _____   _____

Everyday Words

Write each word.

little

funny

7. _____   _____

8. _____   _____

kitten	fish
frog	puppy
dog	pet

Read the clues.

Write the list words.

Two words begin like .

_____   _____

1. _____   2. _____

Two list words rhyme.

_____   _____

3. _____   4. _____

It rhymes with .   It rhymes with ⬭ .

_____   _____

5. _____   6. _____

Write a sentence about a pet.

Use a list word.

_____

7. _____

little	funny

Write the word for each meaning.

_____

8. not big

_____

9. making you laugh

Say a clue for each spelling word, such as, "This is the word for a young cat." Ask your child to write the spelling word that fits your clue.

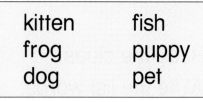

kitten	fish
frog	puppy
dog	pet

Look at the picture.

Write list words to answer the questions.

1. Which pet is a baby dog?

1. _____

_____

2. Which pet hops out of the water?

2. _____

_____

3. Which pet purrs?

3. _____

_____

4. Which pet swims all day?

4. _____

_____

5. Which pet is barking?

5. _____

_____

6. What is a word for each animal?

6. _____

Review

Lesson 19: Long o
Lesson 20: Final e
Lesson 21: Adding -s

Lesson 22: Words to Know
Lesson 23: Animal Words

24

UNIT REVIEW LIST

no	tap	friend	is	kitten
so	tape	friends	are	frog
rode	rip	game	was	dog
nose	ripe	games	were	fish
stone	not	kite	has	puppy
hope	note	kites	had	pet

Word Search

Find the words.
Circle the words.
Write the words you found.

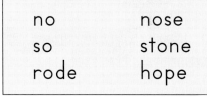

no	nose
so	stone
rode	hope

```
c s o m t n o
a h o p e b f
p z q r o d e
s t o n e g i
d p n o s e u
```

1. _____

2. _____

3. _____

4. _____

5. _____

6. _____

Rhyming Words

Write the word that rhymes with each word.

1. pot

_____

_ _ _ _ _ _ _ _ _ _ _ _ _

_____

2. map

_____

_ _ _ _ _ _ _ _ _ _ _ _ _

_____

3. zip

_____

_ _ _ _ _ _ _ _ _ _ _ _ _

_____

4. vote

_____

_ _ _ _ _ _ _ _ _ _ _ _ _

_____

5. cape

_____

_ _ _ _ _ _ _ _ _ _ _ _ _

_____

6. pipe

_____

_ _ _ _ _ _ _ _ _ _ _ _ _

_____

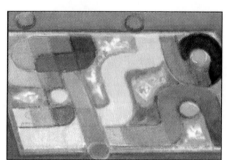

Word Sort

Write the words that go in each list.

friend	games
friends	kite
game	kites

Words that name one person or thing

1. _____

2. _____

3. _____

Words that name more than one person or thing

4. _____

5. _____

6. _____

Missing Letters

Write the missing letters.
Then write the list words.

1.  ___ ___ ___ d   1. _____

2. w ___ r   2. _____

3. h ___ s   3. _____

4. i ___   4. _____

5. w a ___   5. _____

6. a ___ ___   6. _____

Label the Pictures

Write the list word that names each picture.

kitten	fish
frog	puppy
dog	pet

1. _____

2. _____

3. _____

4. _____

5. _____

6. _____

How I Help

Words with cl, sl, st

Look at each word. **Say** it.
Listen for the beginning sounds.
Write each word. **Check** it.

25

class

clay

sled

slip

star

step

1. _____

2. _____

3. _____

4. _____

5. _____

6. _____

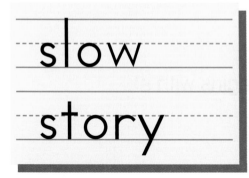
Everyday Words

Write each word.

slow

story

7. _____

8. _____

 Spell each list word aloud and ask your child to say the word. Then say each word and ask your child to spell it.

class	slip
clay	star
sled	step

Write two list words that begin like STOP .

_____   _____

1. _____   2. _____

Write two list words that begin like ☁ .

_____   _____

3. _____   4. _____

Write two list words that begin like 🛝 .

_____   _____

5. _____   6. _____

Write the missing list word.

_____

7. My teacher put a _____ on my paper.

class
clay
sled

slow	story

8. Write the word that begins with **st**.

_____

_____

9. Write the word that begins with **sl**.

_____

_____

class	slip
clay	star
sled	step

Listen for the **cl** in **clay**.
Write **cl** to make new words.

1. _____ ip   2. _____ ap   3. _____ am

Listen for the **st** in **step**.
Write **st** to make new words.

4. _____ ill   5. _____ ay   6. _____ ove

Write a sentence about winter fun.
Use a list word.

7. _____

_____

_____

Write a sentence. Use the word **slow** or **story**.

8. _____

Write two words you want to learn to spell.

_____   _____

Help your child practice for a spelling test. Say each word, use it in a sentence, repeat the word, and have your child write it.

class	slip
clay	star
sled	step

Read about winter fun.
Write the missing list words.

_____

1. Our _____ will go out to play.

_____

2. It is fun to _____ and slide in
the snow.

_____

3. Each _____ makes a footprint.

_____

4. We take turns on the _____ .

_____

5. We use a _____ pot for
the snowman's hat.

_____

6. We make _____ shapes in
the snow.

Words with tr, fr, gr

Look at each word. **Say** it.
Listen for the beginning sounds.
Write each word. **Check** it.

26

train

try

free

fry

grow

grandma

1. _____

2. _____

3. _____

4. _____

5. _____

6. _____

Everyday Words

Write each word.

from

of

7. _____

8. _____

Say each spelling word and ask your child if it begins with **tr, fr,** or **gr.** Then have your child spell the word.

train	fry
try	grow
free	grandma

Write two list words that begin like [frog].

1. _____ 2. _____

Write two list words that begin like [splat].

3. _____ 4. _____

Write two list words that begin like [truck].

5. _____ 6. _____

Write a list word in each shape.

7.

8.

from	of

Write the missing letters. Then write the words.

9. ___ f _____

10. ___ ___ o m _____

train	fry
try	grow
free	grandma

Some words are made from two words.

rain + coat = raincoat

Make one word from two words.

1. grand + ma = _____

2. foot + ball = _____

3. pop + corn = _____

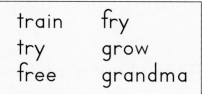

Write a sentence about a visit.
Use a list word.

4. _____

Write a sentence. Use the word **from** or **of** .

5. _____

Write two words for places to visit.

 **MY WORDS** ▶ _____   _____

train	fry
try	grow
free	grandma

Read about a trip.
Write the missing list words.

1. Dad gets tickets for the _____ .

2. The baby rides for _____ .

3. We will _____ to sit together.

4. Our grandpa and _____ pick us up.

5. Grandpa says, "You _____ taller each year."

6. Grandma will _____ fish for our lunch.

Words with ld, nd, st

Look at each word. **Say** it.
Listen for the ending sounds.
Write each word. **Check** it.

27

old

cold

end

send

fast

lost

1. _____

2. _____

3. _____

4. _____

5. _____

6. _____

Everyday Words

Write each word.

best

went

7. _____

8. _____

Say a clue for each spelling word, such as, "This word means the opposite of *young*." Ask your child to write the spelling word that fits your clue.

old	send
cold	fast
end	lost

Write the list words that end with **st**.

1. _____ 2. _____

Write the list words that end with **ld**.

3. _____ 4. _____

Write the list words that end with **nd**.

5. _____ 6. _____

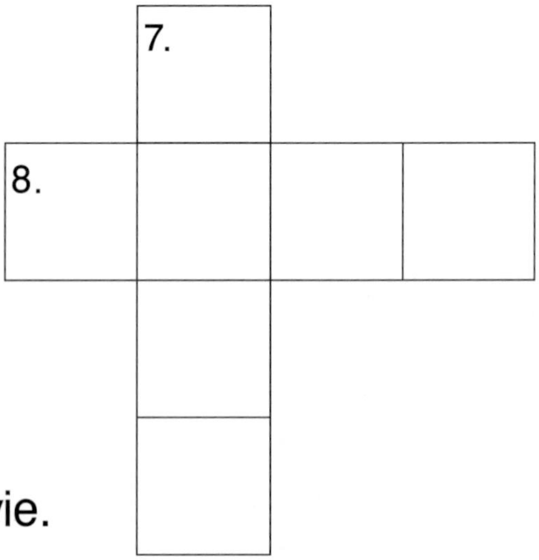

best   went

Write the word for each clue.

7. I ____ to see a movie.

8. It was the ____ movie I ever saw.

Name

old	send
cold	fast
end	lost

Write the letter **t**.

1. †

Do your **t**'s cross on the middle line?
Write **fast** and **lost**.

2. fast

3. lost

Write a sentence about a good story.
Use a list word.

4.

Write a sentence. Use the word **best** or **went** .

5.

Write two words from a good story.

 **MY WORDS**

Write the list words on index cards. Mix the order and ask your child to find the pairs of words that end with the same letters and sounds.

153

Read about Rabbit and Turtle.
Write the missing list words.

old	send
cold	fast
end	lost

1. Rabbit can run _____ .

2. Turtle is _____ , but
he is smart.

3. Rabbit stops for a _____ drink.

4. Turtle is first at the _____ of the race.

5. Please _____ everyone
the news!

6. Rabbit has _____ the race.

Words to Know

Look at each word. **Say** it.
Write each word. **Check** it.

do	1.	
does	2.	
could	3.	
would	4.	
be	5.	
been	6.	

Everyday Words

Write each word.

did	7.	
done	8.	

A shape and a color stand for each letter.
Use this secret code to write the list words.

do	would
does	be
could	been

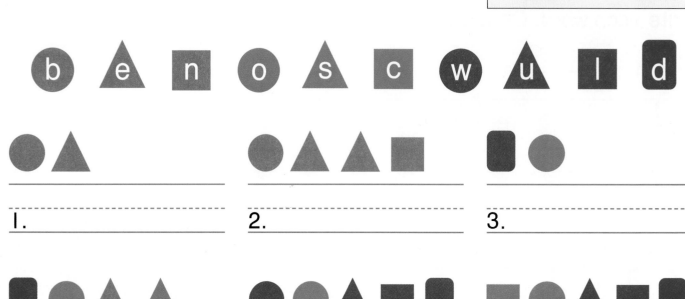

1. _____

2. _____

3. _____

4. _____

5. _____

6. _____

Write the missing list word.

7. He will _____ in bed at nine.

did	done

Write the missing letters.
Then write the words.

8. d __ n __ _____

9. __ id _____

do	would
does	be
could	been

A dictionary shows how to spell words.

do **Do** you like peanuts? I **do**! I will **do** my work tomorrow. **does, did, done, doing**.

does **Does** she like peanuts? Yes, she **does**! He **does** all his work.

Finish the sentences. Check your spelling.

1. We will _____ the job now.

2. He always _____ his work.

Write a sentence about a play. Use a list word.

3. _____

Write a sentence. Use the word **did** or **done** .

4. _____

Write two words that tell about a play.

MY WORDS ➤ _____   _____

 Write each spelling word on an index card. Say the word as you show a card. Hold the card behind you and ask your child to spell the word.

do	would
does	be
could	been

Read about planning a play.
Write the missing list words.

1. Who will _____ the star?

2. Sarah _____ be the princess.

3. Who can help _____ some work?

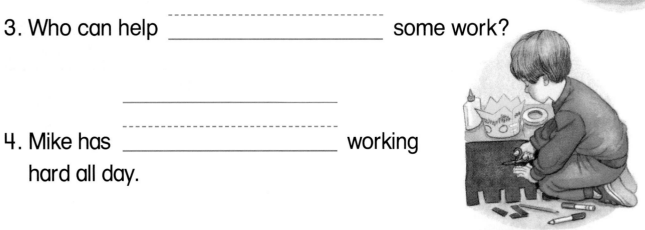

4. Mike has _____ working hard all day.

5. Who _____ like to tell us what to do?

6. Shawn _____ this job well.

Name
....

Family Words

Listen to the poem.

Think about what a family is.

Who are the people in your family?

What is a family?
Who is a family?
Either a lot or a few is a family;
But whether there's ten or
    there's two in *your* family,
All of your family plus *you* is a family!

Mary Ann Hoberman

Read the poem aloud with your child. You may want to talk about what makes your family special.

159

Look at each word. **Say** it.
Listen to its sounds.
Write each word. **Check** it.

mom	1.
dad	2.
brother	3.
sister	4.
baby	5.
family	6.

Everyday Words

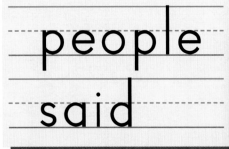

Write each word.

people	7.
said	8.

160

Read the clues.
Write the list words.

mom	sister
dad	baby
brother	family

It begins like .

1. _____

It begins like .

2. _____

It begins like .

3. _____

It begins like 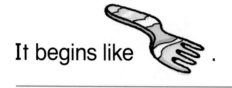.

4. _____

It begins like .

5. _____

It begins like .

6. _____

Write a sentence about your family.
Use a list word.

7. _____

people   said

Write the missing letters. Then write the words.

8. p __ __ __ p l __   _____

9. s __ __ d   _____

Say a clue for each spelling word, such as, "This word means *mother.*" Ask your child to write the spelling word that fits your clue.

Look at the people in this picture.
Write the missing list words.

mom	sister
dad	baby
brother	family

1. The man is the _____ .

2. The woman is the _____ .

3. The girl is the _____ .

4. The boy is the _____ .

5. The little child with the bow is a _____ .

6. The word for all these people is _____ .

Review

Lesson 25: Words with cl, sl, st

Lesson 26: Words with tr, fr, gr

Lesson 27: Words with ld, nd, st

Lesson 28: Words to Know

Lesson 29: Family Words

UNIT REVIEW LIST

class	train	old	do	mom
clay	try	cold	does	dad
sled	free	end	could	brother
slip	fry	send	would	sister
star	grow	fast	be	baby
step	grandma	lost	been	family

Word Sort

Write the words that go in each list.

class	slip
clay	star
sled	step

Words that begin with **sl**

1. _____

2. _____

Words that begin with **st**

3. _____

4. _____

Words that begin with **cl**

5. _____

6. _____

Crossword Puzzles

Write the list word for each clue.

train	fry
try	grow
free	grandma

1. a way to cook food

2. what you can ride
   from place to place

3. get bigger

4. the mother of your
   dad or mom

5. You can do it if you ____ .

6. Something you don't have
   to pay for is ____ .

Missing Words

Write the missing words.

old	send
cold	fast
end	lost

 _____ and Found

 _____ Drinks for Sale

 The _____

1. _____

2. _____

3. _____

 _____ flowers to someone today.

 Recycle _____ newspapers here.

 _____ Food

4. _____

5. _____

6. _____

Missing Letters

Write the missing letters.

do	would
does	be
could	been

1. d _ _ _ s

2. w _ _ _ _ _ d

3. _ _ e

4. b _ _ n

5. c _ _ _ _ d

6. _ _ o

Label the Pictures

Write the list words to label the pictures.

mom	sister
dad	baby
brother	family

1. _____

2. _____

3. _____

4. _____

5. _____

6. Our _____

The Best Day

Words with ch, sh, th, wh

Look at each word. **Say** it.
Listen for the beginning sound.
Write each word. **Check** it.

31

chin

shoe

the

they

when

what

1.

2.

3.

4.

5.

6.

Everyday Words

Write each word.

that

with

7.

8.

Spell each list word aloud and ask your child to say the word. Then say each word and ask your child to spell it.

169

Read the clues. Write the list words.

It begins like 🐚 .   It begins like 🪑 .

_____   _____

1. _____   2. _____

Two words begin like ⚙ .

_____   _____

3. _____   4. _____

Two words begin like | that | .

_____   _____

5. _____   6. _____

| that | with |

Read the sentences. Write the missing words in the puzzle.

7. We must look for ____ pen.

8. Come ____ us.

chin	they
shoe	when
the	what

A dictionary tells what words mean.

> **nice**   **Nice** means good or kind. I had a **nice** time.
> It was **nice** of you to help me. **nicer, nicest.**

Write the list word that goes with each
dictionary meaning.

1. something you wear
   on your foot

   _____

   - - - - - - - - - - -

   _____

2. the part of the face
   below the mouth

   _____

   - - - - - - - - - - -

   _____

Write a sentence about a favorite rhyme.
Use a list word.

3. _____

   -

   _____

Write a sentence. Use the word **that** or **with** .

_____

- -

4. _____

Write two words you can find in a dictionary.

 **MY WORDS**

_____   _____

- - - - - - - - - - -   - - - - - - - - - - -

_____   _____

Help your child practice for a spelling test. Say each word, use it in a sentence, repeat the word, and have your child write it.

171

You may know a rhyme that is a little like this one. Write the missing list words.

chin	they
shoe	when
the	what

1. There was an old woman

   _____

   who lived in a _____ .

2. She had many children

   _____

   and knew _____ to do.

   _____

3. When _____ were hungry,

   she fed them some bread.

   _____

4. And _____ one was good,

   _____

   she patted him on _____ head.

5. She gave one child a hug and a grin when

   _____

   he fell down and hurt his _____ .

Adding -ed

Some words tell what happens now.
Add **-ed** to tell what happened in the past.
Look at each word. **Say** it.
Write each word. **Check** it.

play

played

help

helped

rest

rested

1.

2.

3.

4.

5.

6.

Everyday Words

Write each word.

want

too

7.

8.

play	helped
played	rest
help	rested

Write the list words that end with **-ed.**
Then circle the list word that is in each
word you wrote.

_____ _____ _____
1. _____ 2. _____ 3. _____

Write the list words you circled.

_____ _____ _____
4. _____ 5. _____ 6. _____

Write the missing list words.

_____

7. The boy wants to _____
   the teacher.

_____

8. He _____ her yesterday too.

want	too

Write the word to finish each sentence.

_____

9. I _____ to play.

_____

10. She wants to play _____ .

A word can tell about what happens now.
We **help** our mom.

Add **-ed** to tell what happened in the past.
We **helped** our mom last night.

play	helped
played	rest
help	rested

Add **-ed** to the underlined word in each sentence.
Write the new word.

1. Let's <u>rest</u> now.

   _____

   We _____ at noon.

2. Let's <u>play</u> baseball.

   _____

   We _____ yesterday.

Write a sentence about a place where you play.

3. _____
   _____
   _____

Write a sentence. Use the word **want** or **too** .

4. _____
   _____

Write two words that tell what you can do at a park.

 _____ _____

_____ _____

Read about a soccer game.
Write the missing list words.

play	helped
played	rest
help	rested

1. Have you ever _____ soccer?

2. Would you like to _____
   with us now?

3. We can _____ you learn to play.

4. Everyone _____ our team win!

5. Now let's sit down to _____ .

6. We will play again when
   we have _____ .

Adding -ing

Sometimes you add **-ing** to words that tell
what is happening.
Look at each word. **Say** it.
Write each word. **Check** it.

33

go

going

sleep

sleeping

hold

holding

1. _____

2. _____

3. _____

4. _____

5. _____

6. _____

Everyday Words

Write each word.

know

once

7. _____

8. _____

 Write *go*, *sleep*, *hold*, and *-ing* on index cards. Ask your child to use the cards to make three words that end in **-ing.**   177

go	sleeping
going	hold
sleep	holding

Write the list words that end with **-ing**.
Then circle the list word that is in each
word you wrote.

1. _____ 2. _____ 3. _____

Write the list words you circled.

4. _____ 5. _____ 6. _____

Read the clues. Write the list words.

It rhymes with **cold**.   It rhymes with **jeep**.   It rhymes with **no**.

7. _____ 8. _____ 9. _____

know	once

Write the word that goes with each meaning.

10. one time

_____

11. to have facts about something

_____

go	sleeping
going	hold
sleep	holding

Circle each list word that is spelled wrong.
Then write the sentences correctly.

1. We will slep in tents.

2. Please hode the ball.

Write a sentence about going to a place.
Use a list word.

3.

Write a sentence.
Use the word **know** or **once** .

4.

Write two words that you want to learn to spell.

 **MY WORDS**

Print each spelling word on a small piece of paper. Fold the papers and put them in a box. Have your child choose a paper without looking at it. Ask your child to spell that word. Continue until all have been spelled.

179

Read about a day at the beach.
Write the missing list words.

go	sleeping
going	hold
sleep	holding

1. My sister will _____ in the shade.

2. I will not be _____ .

3. I will make a wall to _____ back the water.

4. The wall is _____ back the water.

5. A dog is _____ to knock over

my castle!

6. Dog, _____ play

someplace else!

Words to Know

Look at each word. **Say** it.
Write each word. **Check** it.

34

| her |
| I |
| their |
| his |
| him |
| our |

1.
2.
3.
4.
5.
6.

Write each word.

| you |
| very |

7.
8.

Ask your child to find and circle the list words in a magazine or newspaper.

her	his
I	him
their	our

Find and circle the list words.
Then write the words.

m   v   I   x   y

t   h   e   i   r

s   i   b   q   o

p   s   c   z   u

l   x   h   e   r

h   i   m   g   n

1. _____   2. _____

3. _____   4. _____

5. _____   6. _____

Write the words that begin like   .

7. _____   8. _____   9. _____

| you | very |

Write the missing letters.
Then write the words.

10. v __ __ y   _____

11. y __ __   _____

her	his
I	him
their	our

Write the letter **h**.

1. h

Do your **h**'s start at the top line?
Write **her** and **his**.

2. her

3. his

Write a sentence about something you
like to do. Use a list word.

4.

Write a sentence. Use the word **you** or **very** .

5.

Write words for two of your favorite places.

Cover the bottom of a small pan with sand or salt. Have your child use a finger to write each word in the sand or salt.

her   his
I   him
their   our

Read about a visit to a museum.
Write the missing list words.

1. I visit my aunt and uncle. We go to a museum

   _____

   in _____ neighborhood.

2. My aunt says the museum is

   _____

   _____ favorite place.

3. My uncle says the dinosaurs are

   _____

   _____ favorite thing to see.

4. I ask _____ to show
   me his favorite dinosaurs.

5. _____ like the
   Tyrannosaurus best of all.

6. We all like _____ visit
   to the museum.

Place Words

Listen to the poem.
Do you have a favorite place?

Keziah

I have a secret place to go.
Not anyone may know.

And sometimes when the wind is rough
I cannot get there fast enough.

And sometimes when my mother
Is scolding my big brother,

My secret place, it seems to me,
Is quite the only place to be.

Gwendolyn Brooks

 Read the poem aloud with your child. You may want to talk about favorite places and what makes them special.

Look at each word. **Say** it.
Listen to its sounds.
Write each word. **Check** it.

beach

home

store

school

park

outside

1.

2.

3.

4.

5.

6.

Everyday Words

Write each word.

house

yard

7.

8.

beach	school
home	park
store	outside

Write the word that names each picture.

1. _____

2. _____

3. _____

4. _____

5. _____

6. _____

Write a sentence about a place. Use a list word.

7. _____

_____

_____

house	yard

Write the word for each clue.

8. the ground next to a house _____

9. a place to live _____

Say a clue for each spelling word, such as, "You would find sand at this place." Ask your child to write the spelling word that fits your clue.

187

beach	school
home	park
store	outside

Read the clues about places.
Write the list word to name each place.

1. Name a place to buy clothes and food.

1. _____

2. Name a place to live with your family.

2. _____

3. Name a place with sand and water.

3. _____

4. Name a place to learn to read and write.

4. _____

5. Name a place to play on swings.

5. _____

6. Name a place that is not inside.

6. _____

Review

Lesson 31: Words with ch, sh, th, wh

Lesson 32: Adding -ed

Lesson 33: Adding -ing

Lesson 34: Words to Know

Lesson 35: Place Words

UNIT REVIEW LIST

chin	play	go	her	beach
shoe	played	going	I	home
the	help	sleep	their	store
they	helped	sleeping	his	school
when	rest	hold	him	park
what	rested	holding	our	outside

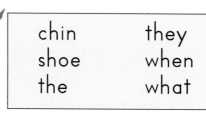

Word Search

Find the words. Circle the words.
Write the words you found.

chin	they
shoe	when
the	what

```
c  t  h  e  z  b  t

h  w  h  a  t  d  h

i  w  h  e  n  q  e

n  m  s  h  o  e  y
```

1. _____

2. _____

3. _____

4. _____

5. _____

6. _____

Proofreading

Circle each list word that is spelled wrong.
Then write the sentences correctly.

play	helped
played	rest
help	rested

1. I like to pla.

_____

_____

2. I plaed at the park.

_____

_____

3. I can hlp my dad.

_____

_____

4. I helpt him work outside.

_____

_____

5. I will rast now.

_____

_____

6. I restid after school.

_____

_____

Label the Pictures

Write two words that tell about each picture.

go	sleeping
going	hold
sleep	holding

1. _____

3. _____

5. _____

2. _____

4. _____

6. _____

Missing Words

Write the missing list words.

her	his
I	him
their	our

1. _____ cap

2. _____ shoe

3. _____

4. for _____

5. _____ dog

6. _____ home

More Missing Words

Write the missing words.

beach	school
home	park
store	outside

Toy _____

1. _____

Home
sweet
_____

2. _____

Public

_____

3. _____

West _____

4. _____

Please
wait
_____.

5. _____

Keep this
_____
clean.

6. _____

When I Grow Up

You may want to talk to your child about the occupations pictured and the occupations of people your child knows.

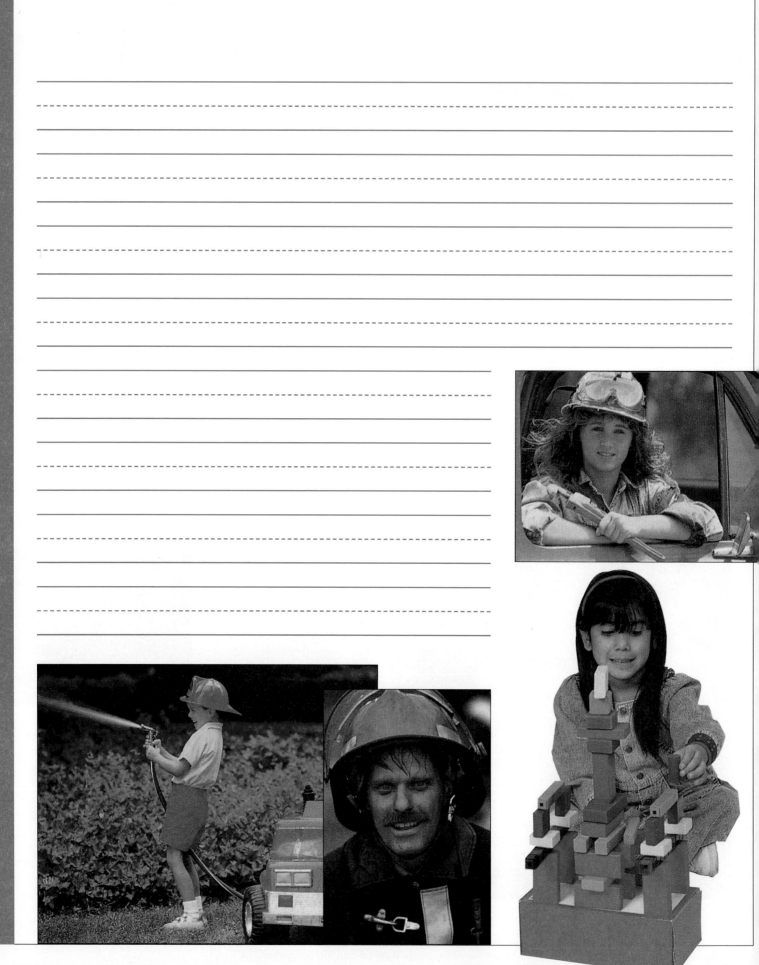

Here I am.

8

What I Like

My name is

_____

_ _ _ _ _ _ _ _ _ _ _ _ _ _ _ _ _ _

_____ .

1

I like

cars

dolls

tacos

hot dogs

grilled cheese

6

3

I like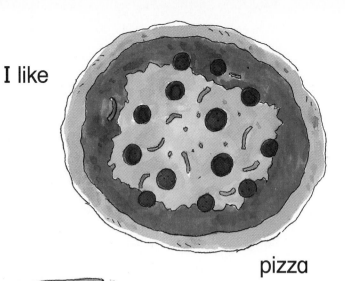

pizza

peanut butter and jelly

2

puzzles

stuffed animals

books

7

I like to

ride a bike

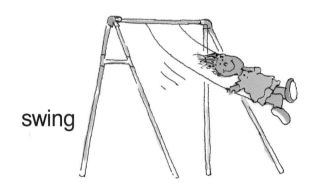

swing

4

swim

paint

skate

5

The Birthday Page

January

February

March

April

May

June

My name is

_____

- - - - - - - - - - - - - - - - - -

_____ .

My birthday is

_____

- - - - - - - - -

_____ .

July

August

September

October

November

December

Children Around the World

Cut out the cards.

Show your friend a word.

Ask your friend to show you the number.

Bonus Page 3 Use for United Nations Day, October 24, or with Unit 2, Lesson 11 Number Words.

199

two	one
four	three
six	five
eight	seven
ten	nine

Name

Thanksgiving Feast

What do you eat for Thanksgiving dinner?

Draw your favorite Thanksgiving food.

turkey

gravy

stuffing

potatoes

salad

beans

bread

pie

My Thanksgiving Menu

Here Comes Winter

Color the picture.

Use the colors that go with the numbers.

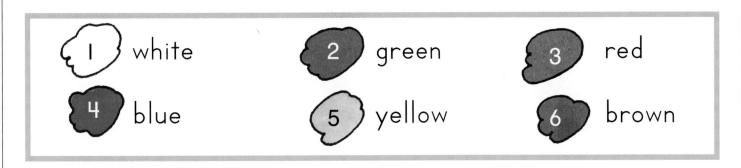

1 white	2 green	3 red
4 blue	5 yellow	6 brown

Bonus Page 5 Use to mark the beginning of winter or with Unit 3, Lesson 17 Color Words.

203

What is winter like where you live?
Draw a picture.

Write a sentence about your picture.

Martin Luther King, Jr. Day

Martin Luther King was a great leader.

He wanted to make the world a better place.

He wanted laws to be fair.

Dr. King dreamed of love and peace for all people.

He worked hard for his dream.

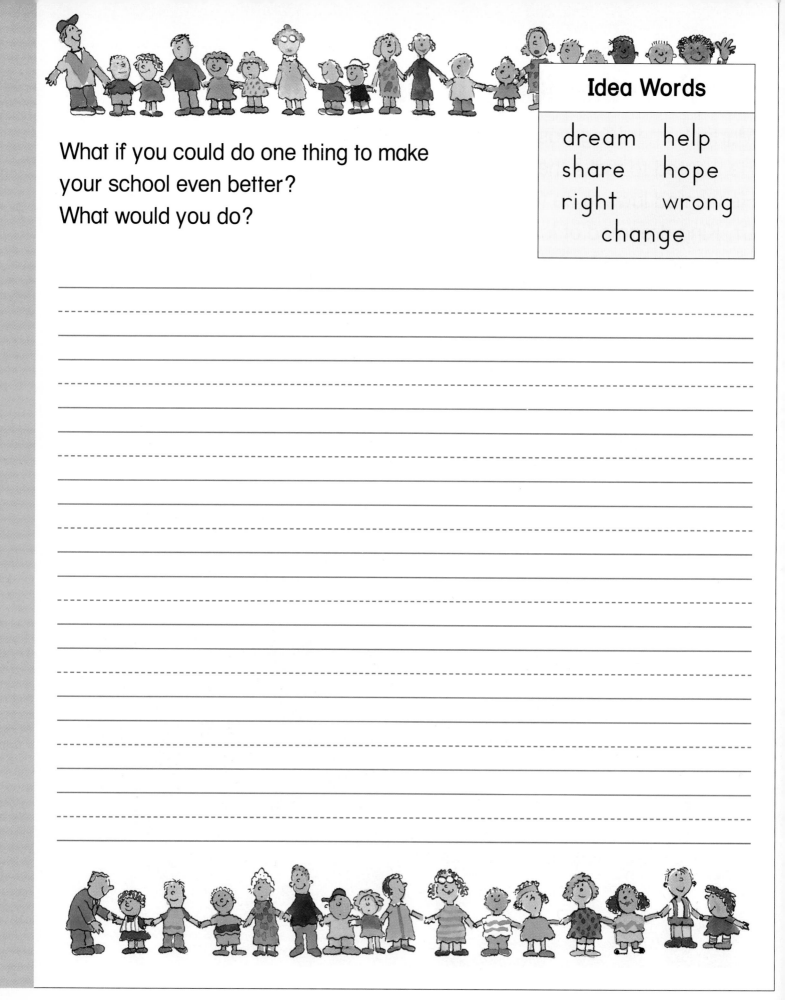

What if you could do one thing to make
your school even better?
What would you do?

Idea Words

dream   help
share   hope
right   wrong
change

Groundhog Day

Help the groundhog find its way out of its den.

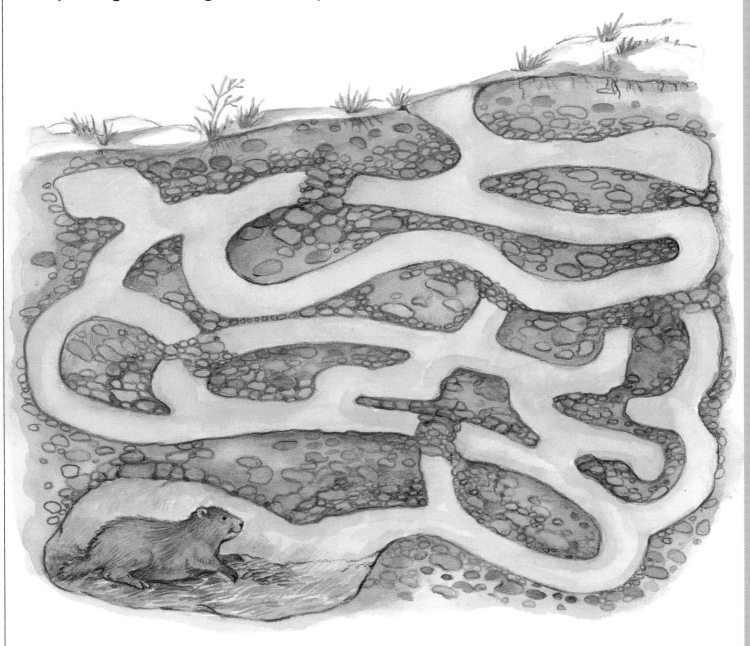

Did this groundhog see its shadow? _____

yes   no

Tell why you think so.

Help the animals find their homes.
Draw a line from each animal to its home.

bat

pond

bee

cave

frog

hive

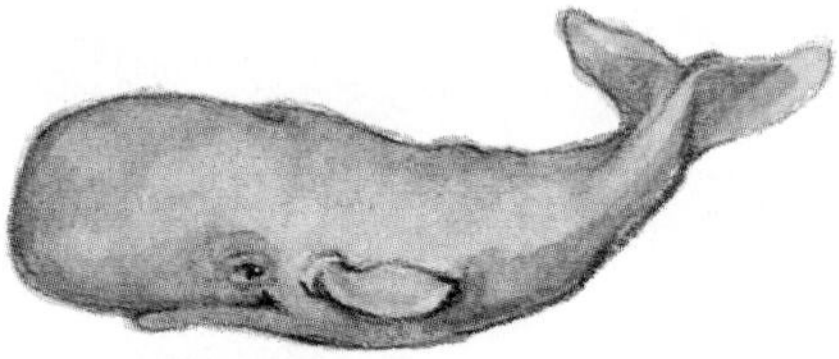

whale

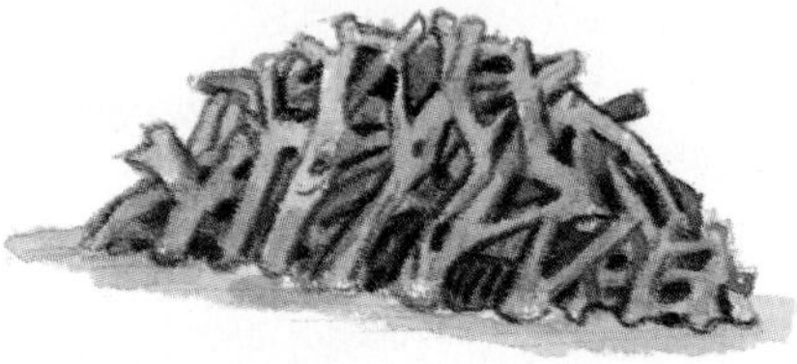

lodge

beaver

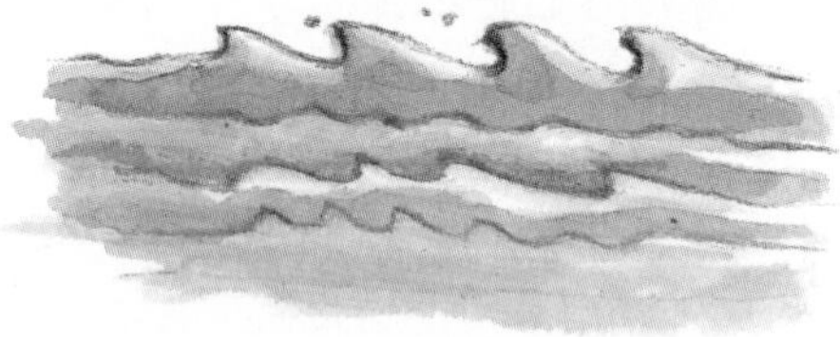

ocean

Pick an animal.
Write one fact about it.

_____

_____

_____

_____

_____

Name

Presidents' Day

Two great American presidents had birthdays in February.
George Washington was born on February 22, 1732.
Abraham Lincoln was born on February 12, 1809.

Here is a birthday game you can play.
How many words can you find in their names?

Bonus Page 8 Use for Presidents' Day or anytime in Unit 4.

209

Abe Lincoln

_____

- - - - - - - - - - - - - - - - -

_____

- - - - - - - - - - - - - - - - -

_____

- - - - - - - - - - - - - - - - -

_____

- - - - - - - - - - - - - - - - -

_____

- - - - - - - - - - - - - - - - -

_____

Ask Your Family

Take these questions home.

Ask each person in your home to answer them.

Tell them to write **yes** or **no** in the boxes.

	Person 1	Person 2	Person 3	Person 4
1. Do you like to read?				
2. Do you like to watch TV?				
3. Do you like to go to movies?				
4. Do you like to dance?				
5. Do you like to listen to music?				

Bonus Page 9 Use with Unit 5, Lesson 29 Family Words, or anytime in Unit 5.

211

	Person 1	Person 2	Person 3	Person 4
6. Do you like to play sports?				
7. Do you like to ride a bike?				
8. Do you like to cook?				
9. Do you like roller coasters?				
10. Do you like to go to the mall?				

What does your family like to do most?

_____

- -

_____

A Helping Hand

What can you do for someone you love?

Write one way you will help.

Cut out the helping hand.

Give it to someone you love.

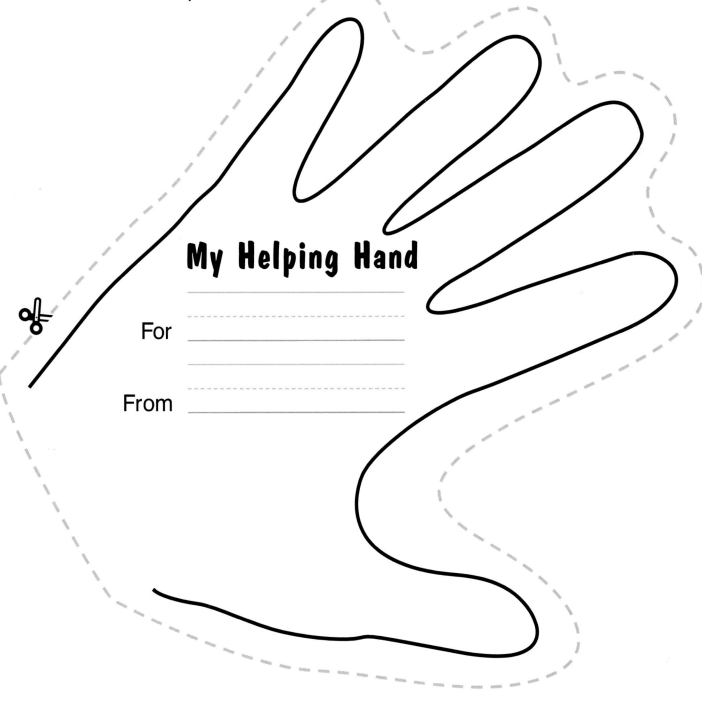

My Helping Hand

For

From

Bonus Page 10 Use for Mother's Day, Father's Day, or anytime in Unit 5.

213

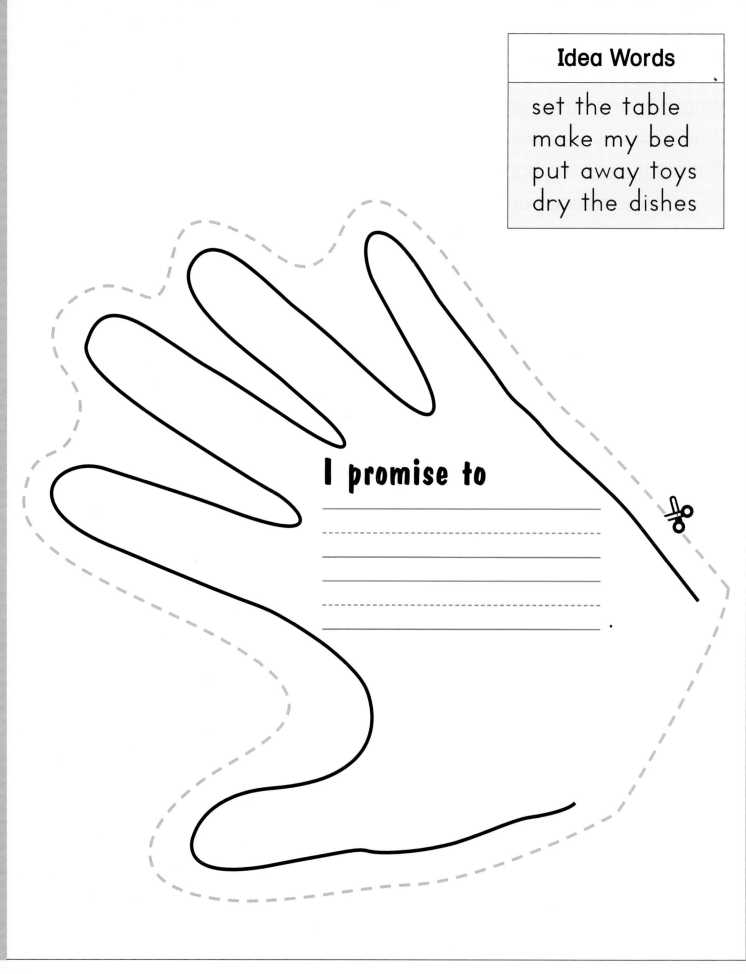

Idea Words

set the table
make my bed
put away toys
dry the dishes

I promise to

_____

- - - - - - - - - - - - - - -

_____

- - - - - - - - - - - - - - -

_____ .

Plan a Field Trip

Read about the museum.

Look at the map on the back.

Circle the things you want to see.

The Rain Forest

Walk through a rain forest.

Listen to the animals.

Dinosaur Hall

When did dinosaurs live?

How big were they?

Find out everything you want
to know about dinosaurs.

American Indian Life

Visit an Indian tepee.

Hold an Indian bow.

Hear about everyday life.

Spiders All Around

Spiders are everywhere!

Are they dangerous?

You can find out here.

Space Travel

See moon rocks and spacesuits.

Try flying a spaceship.

Can you land it on the moon?

The Story of Cars

How did the first car look?

What is the fastest car ever made?

This is the place to learn all
about cars.

What would you see first?

_____

_____

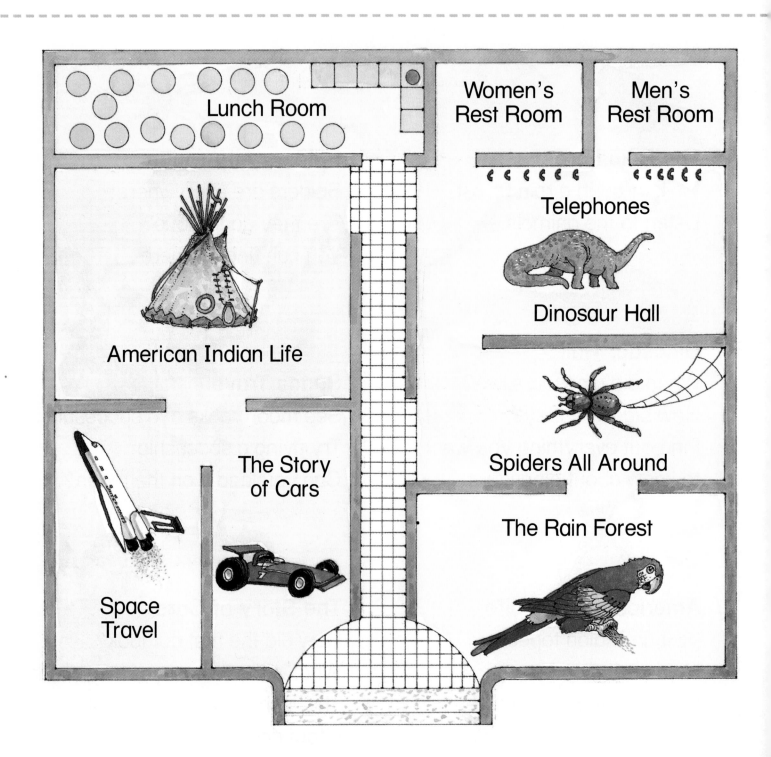

Name _____

My First Grade
Memory Book

To Mrs. Brown

1

Autographs

4

Bonus Page 12 Use for the last day of school or anytime in Unit 6.

217

These were the best things
about First Grade.

The best subject was

_____

_____

_____

The best teacher was

_____

_____

_____

My best friend was

_____

_____

_____

The best book was

_____

_____

_____

The best song was

_____

_____

_____

The best game was

_____

_____

_____

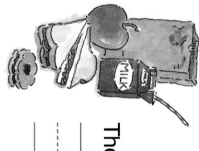

The best lunch was

_____

_____

_____

Spelling Dictionary

You can look up your spelling words in this Spelling Dictionary. This page shows what you will find if you look up **hit.** It can help you when you look up a word.

This is the word you are looking up. The words in a dictionary are in ABC order.

A sentence tells you the meaning of the word.

hit

hit Hit means to push hard against something. Jenny **hit** the ball with her bat. The car **hit** a tree. **hit, hitting.**

Extra forms of the word come at the end.

A sentence shows how the word is used.

Sometimes a picture helps show the meaning of the word.

A

a Pat has **a** red hat. Do you have **a** book on cats? Thanksgiving comes once **a** year.

am Today I **am** seven years old.

an There is **an** apple in the basket, and a banana too. I ate **an** egg and two pieces of toast.

and His hat **and** mittens are blue. 4 **and** 2 make 6. Sue **and** Lee played a game.

are You **are** right. We **are** ready. They **are** waiting for us.

as Emily ran **as** fast **as** she could to win the race.

at The boy is **at** the chalkboard. The dog barked **at** the cat.

ate We **ate** our lunch in the park.

ate

B

baby A **baby** is a very young child. Little **babies** can't walk. **babies.**

baby

bat¹ A **bat** is used to hit the ball in baseball. **bats.**

bat¹

bat² A **bat** is a small animal that flies. Its face is like that of a mouse. Its wings are covered with skin. **Bats** fly around at night. **bats.**

bat²

be He wants to **be** an artist when he grows up. Will Erin and Jason **be** at the party?

beach A **beach** is an area of land next to the water. **Beaches** are covered with sand or stones. **beaches.**

bed A **bed** is something to sleep on. What time do you go to **bed?** Mom put the baby in her **bed. beds.**

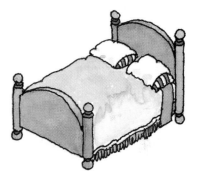

bed

been You can tell that Nicole and Joe have **been** playing in the mud. Have you **been** to the circus?

best His work is good. Your work is better, but her work is **best.**

big If something is **big,** it has great size. Something **big** is not little. Jerry has a **big** dog. Lita's dog is **bigger** than Jerry's. It is the **biggest** I have ever seen. **bigger, biggest.**

big   bigger

bike

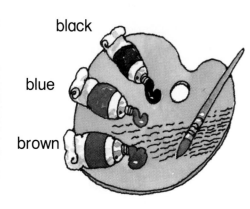

black

blue

brown

bike Bike is another word for bicycle. A **bike** has two wheels. You ride it by pushing the pedals. **bikes.**

black Black is a color. The words in this book are printed in **black.**

blue Blue is a color. On a clear day the sky is **blue.**

box A **box** has four sides and a bottom. A **box** can also have a top. We use **boxes** to hold things. **boxes.**

brother Your **brother** is a boy who has the same mother and father that you have. Sam has a big **brother** and a little sister. **brothers.**

brown Brown is a color. Toast and chocolate are **brown.**

bus A **bus** is like a big car with many seats. A **bus** carries people from place to place. A school **bus** takes children to school. **buses.**

bus

but You may look at the flowers, **but** you must not pick them. We wanted to go swimming **but** we couldn't.

by The playground is **by** the school. The tree house was built **by** Ann and her friends.

C

came   He **came** to the party early.

cat   A **cat** is a small animal with soft fur. **Cats** are often kept as pets. **cats.**

cat

chin   The **chin** is the part of the face below the mouth. **chins.**

class   A **class** is a group of boys and girls who learn together. Most schools have many **classes. classes.**

chin

clay   **Clay** is a kind of earth. Wet **clay** can be shaped into pots and dishes. **Clay** gets hard when it dries.

cold   I **Cold** means not hot. Winter weather can be **cold. colder, coldest.**
2 **Cold** also means a kind of sickness. You cough and sneeze when you have a **cold.** Many people get **colds** in the winter. **colds.**

come   Can you **come** to my birthday party? My dad will **come** at six o'clock. **came, come, coming.**

could   Her brother said he **could** come. When Grandpa was young, he **could** dance well.

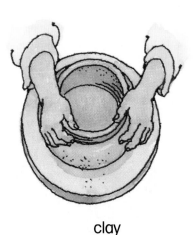
clay

cry

cup

cry 1 **Cry** means to call loudly. He **cried,** "Look out!"
2 **Cry** also means to have tears come from the eyes.
Babies **cry** when they are hungry. **cried, crying.**

cup A **cup** is a dish to drink from. **Cups** are round and
deep. You can drink milk from a **cup. cups.**

cut When you **cut** something, you divide it into pieces.
Dad **cut** the meat with a knife. Juan used scissors to
cut the paper. **cut, cutting.**

cut

D

dad **Dad** is a short name for father. A **dad** is a man
who has a child or children. **dads.**

day 1 **Day** is the time when the sun is up. **Days** are
brighter and warmer than nights.
2 A **day** is also 24 hours of light and dark. There
are seven **days** in a week. **days.**

did Yoshio **did** a good job taking care of his dog.
Did you see Carlos today?

dig

dig **Dig** means to make a hole in the ground. The dog
dug a place to hide its bone. **dug, digging.**

do **Do** you like peanuts? I **do**! I will **do** my work tomorrow. **does, did, done, doing.**

does **Does** she like peanuts? Yes, she **does**! He **does** all his work.

dog A **dog** is an animal. Some **dogs** are big and some are small. Many people keep **dogs** as pets. **dogs.**

done She has **done** all her work. Have you **done** all your work?

E

end **End** means the last part of something. Don is at the **end** of the line. Did you read the **end** of the story? **ends.**

end

F

family A mother, a father, and their children make up a **family**. **Family** also means cousins, aunts, uncles, and grandparents. **families.**

fast 1 **Fast** means quick. She is a **fast** runner. 2 When you go **fast**, you go in a quick way. Some boats go very **fast**. **faster, fastest.**

feed **Feed** means to give food to someone. It's time to **feed** the baby. Adam **fed** the dog. **fed, feeding.**

feed

fish A **fish** is an animal that lives in the water. There are many kinds of **fish**. Some kinds live in the ocean. Some live in lakes and rivers. **fish.**

fish

five **Five** is the number 5. **Five** is one more than four. **fives.**

for She went to the store **for** milk. We went **for** a swim. This orange is **for** you.

four **Four** is the number 4. **Four** is one more than three. **fours.**

free

free 1 **Free** means loose, or not shut up. She set the bird **free** from the cage.
2 When something is **free,** you do not have to pay money for it. The show in the park is **free.**

friend A **friend** is someone you like and who likes you. It is nice to have **friends. friends.**

friend

frog A **frog** is a small animal with long back legs. **Frogs** jump from place to place. Most **frogs** live near water. **frogs.**

frog

from   Is Mary home **from** school? Billy took a book **from** the table. Three weeks **from** today is David's birthday.

fry   **Fry** means to cook in hot fat. He loves to eat **fried** chicken for dinner. **fried, frying.**

fun   When you have **fun,** you have a good time. The children had **fun** on the swing.

funny   When something is **funny,** it makes you laugh. The children laughed at the **funny** clown. **funnier, funniest.**

G

game   A **game** is something you can play. Children like to play **games. games.**

gave   Bob **gave** his mother a flower.

get   Sam hopes to **get** presents on his birthday. When I **get** home, I eat a snack. Mom **gets** up early. **got, gotten, getting.**

go   **Go** means to move from one place to another. Roger likes to **go** to the store. He **goes** there every day. That car is **going** fast. **went, gone, going.**

got   She **got** ice skates for her birthday.

grandma   **Grandma** means grandmother. A **grandma** is the mother of your father or mother. **grandmas.**

got

grandma

227

green

green **Green** is a color. Grass and leaves are **green** in the summer.

grow **Grow** means to get bigger. Children **grow** every year. The sunflower is **growing** fast. **grew, grown, growing.**

grow

H

had Pat **had** a cold. He **had** to stay in bed.

has Pat still **has** a cold. He **has** to stay in bed. Kate **has** a new dog.

have Pat and I both **have** colds. We **have** to stay in bed. The Burkes **have** a new TV. **has, had, having.**

he Who is **he? He** is my friend, Lee. **He** likes to sing.

help When you **help** someone, you do something useful for them. Tom **helped** his mother wash the car. **helped, helping.**

her I like **her.** I do not like **her** dog. Give **her** the book.

him I like **him.** I gave **him** my apple. When did you give it to **him?**

his **His** name is Marco. This is **his** dog. My dog is young, but **his** is old.

her

hit   **Hit** means to push hard against something. Jenny **hit** the ball with her bat. The car **hit** a tree. **hit, hitting.**

hold   I To **hold** something is to take it in your hands or arms. Please **hold** my coat. Nick **held** the baby. **2 Hold** also means to have space for something. This big glass **holds** a lot of water. **held, holding.**

home   Your **home** is the place where you live. Gail's **home** is on Oak Street. **homes.**

hop   **Hop** means to jump. The rabbit **hopped** away. Luz **hops** on one foot. **hopped, hopping.**

hope   **Hope** means you want something to happen. I **hope** you are well soon. **hoped, hoping.**

hot   When something is **hot,** it is very, very warm. A sunny day in August can be **hot.** Fire is **hot.** Do not touch the **hot** stove. **hotter, hottest.**

hit

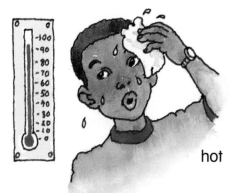

hop

hot

house   A **house** is a building where people live. Mary's **house** is in the city. Nick's **house** is in the country. **houses.**

house

in

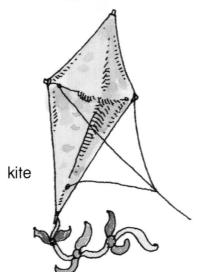

kite

kitten

I

I **I** watched television last night.

in The brown cat is **in** the house, and the black cat is out. It is cold here **in** winter. Be home **in** time for lunch. Please come **in.**

is Her dog **is** outside. **Is** it starting to rain?

it **It** is nine o'clock in the morning. Is **it** too early to telephone Jack? My ball is at his house and I need **it.**

K

kite A **kite** is a toy that you fly with a string. Most **kites** are made of light wood and paper. We like to fly **kites. kites.**

kitten A **kitten** is a baby cat. **kittens.**

know **Know** means to have facts about someone or something. Do you **know** how to swim? Julie **knows** everyone in her class. **knew, known, knowing.**

L

late **Late** means after the usual time. Hurry or you'll be **late** for school. **later, latest.**

led She **led** the children across the street. We were **led** into the cave by a guide.

like[1] **Like** means the same as. My toy is just **like** yours.

like[1]

like[2] **Like** means to be pleased with something or someone. Most people **like** apple pie. I **like** all my friends. **liked, liking.**

little If something is **little,** it is not big. His pet is a **little** kitten. **littler, littlest.**

lost Luis **lost** his money.

lost

M

made Mother **made** lemonade.

make 1 **Make** means to put together or build something. Let's **make** a boat. She **made** a cake. 2 **Make** also means to cause something to take place. Thunder **makes** a loud noise. You **make** me laugh. **made, making.**

make

man A boy grows up to be a **man.** Boys grow up to be **men. men.**

may **May** we go outside to play? We **may** go to the circus tonight.

me He saw **me** at the swimming pool. The secret is between you and **me.**

met We **met** our friends at the park.

mom

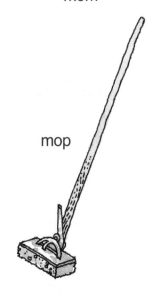
mop

mom Mom is another name for mother. A **mom** is a woman who has a child or children. **moms.**

mop You use a **mop** to clean the floor. A **mop** has a long handle. **mops.**

my I lost **my** mittens in the park. I was playing with **my** friends.

N

never I have **never** met a monster. I hope I **never** will.

nice Nice means good or kind. I had a **nice** time. It was **nice** of you to help me. **nicer, nicest.**

no There are **no** oranges left. Just say **no** if you don't want to play.

nose Your **nose** is in the middle of your face. **Noses** help us smell things. **noses.**

nose

not I am **not** surprised. It's **not** time to leave. Brett is **not** at home.

note A **note** is a very short letter. My aunt sent me a **note** on my birthday. **notes.**

O

of This book **of** mine is all about monsters. My toy dinosaur is made **of** plastic.

old Someone who is **old** has lived for a long time. My grandmother is **old** and I am young. **older, oldest.**

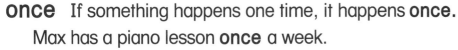

old

on The paper is **on** the desk. The TV is **on.** I talked to Bill **on** the phone. I put my hat **on.**

once If something happens one time, it happens **once.** Max has a piano lesson **once** a week.

one One is the number 1. Which **one** do you want? **ones.**

or I can play outside with my football **or** inside with my pet bird. Hurry up **or** you will be late.

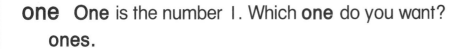

on

our **Our** garden looked beautiful, but their garden did not.

outside Mom and Jessica waited **outside** for the mail carrier to come. The **outside** of the carrot was dirty so we had to wash it.

P

park 1 A **park** is an area of land with grass and trees. People can use **parks** for walking and playing. Some **parks** have playgrounds. **parks.**
2 **Park** also means to leave a car someplace for a time. Mother **parked** the car in the garage. **parked, parking.**

park

pen A **pen** is used for writing. **Pens** are often made of plastic. There is ink in a **pen. pens.**

pen

people

people Men, women, and children are **people.** There were many **people** at the picnic.

pet A **pet** is a favorite animal that you take care of. Gina has both a cat and a dog as **pets. pets.**

pin A **pin** is used to hold things together. It has one sharp end to stick through things. **pins.**

play 1 **Play** means to have fun. Let's **play** after school. **played, playing.**
2 **Play** also means a story that is acted. Carol is in her class **play. plays.**

play

pot A **pot** is used to hold things. Some **pots** are for cooking. Some **pots** hold plants or flowers. Dad made a big **pot** of soup. **pots.**

pot

puppy A **puppy** is a baby dog. **puppies.**

R

ran Jill **ran** all the way home.

red **Red** is a color. Strawberries are **red.** Dana's wagon is bright **red.**

red

rest I When you **rest,** you stay quiet. After playing hard, Angela **rested. rested, resting.**
2 **Rest** also means the part that is left. Would you like the **rest** of this fruit?

ride When you **ride** something, it carries you along. Jill is **riding** her bike. Tom **rode** a horse. **rode, ridden, riding.**

ride

rip I If you **rip** something, you tear it in a rough way. He didn't want to **rip** his drawing. She **ripped** the paper off the gift. **ripped, ripping.**
2 A **rip** is a torn place. I will sew up the **rip** in my jeans. **rips.**

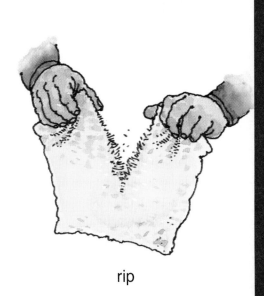
rip

ripe **Ripe** corn is ready to be picked and eaten.

rode I **rode** my bike to school.

s

said   She **said** she would help us.

say   When you **say** something, you are speaking out loud. Did Tyler **say** he would be late? **said, saying.**

school   **School** is a place where you learn things. We learn to read in **school. schools.**

see   When you **see** something, you look at it with your eyes. Did you **see** the red bird? **saw, seen, seeing.**

send   **Send** means to cause someone or something to go from one place to another. **I sent** her a letter. Dad **sent** me out to play. **sent, sending.**

seven   **Seven** is the number 7. **Seven** is one more than six. **sevens.**

she   Who is **she? She** is my teacher.

shoe   A **shoe** is something you wear on your foot. Kristin's **shoes** are black, and Kyle's **shoes** are brown. **shoes.**

sister   Your **sister** is a girl who has the same mother and father that you have. Maria has a **sister. sisters.**

sit   When you **sit,** you rest on the lower part of your body with knees bent. We **sat** in our chairs. **sat, sitting.**

six   **Six** is the number 6. **Six** is one more than five. **sixes.**

shoe

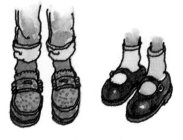

sister

sit

sled   A **sled** is used to slide on snow or ice. We used our **sled** after the first heavy snow this winter. **sleds.**

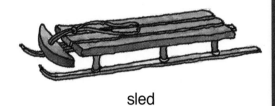

sled

sleep   I **Sleep** means to rest your body. April had a dream last night when she was **sleeping. slept, sleeping.**
2 **Sleep** also means the rest your body needs each night. I try to get eight hours of **sleep** every night.

slip   **Slip** means to slide and fall. Mark **slipped** on the ice and broke his arm. **slipped, slipping.**

slow   I Something that is **slow** takes a long time. When something is **slow,** it is not fast. The **slow** runner lost the race. **slower, slowest.**
2 If you **slow** down, you take longer to do things. Al **slowed** down when Bob could not keep up with him. **slowed, slowing.**

slip

so   The dog seemed hungry, **so** we fed it. I was **so** tired I fell asleep.

some   **Some** of the children jumped rope. **Some** animals make good pets.

star   I A **star** is something that shines in the sky at night. **Stars** are very far away from the earth.
2 A **star** is also a shape that has five or more points. My teacher drew a **star** on my paper. **stars.**

star

star

237

step 1 Each time you move your foot as you go from place to place, you take a **step**. It is just a few **steps** from here to the kitchen.

2 A **step** is also the place you put your feet when you walk up and down stairs. Billy reached the top **step** without falling. **steps.**

step

stone A **stone** is a small piece of rock. The children threw **stones** into the pond. **stones.**

store A **store** is a place to buy things. We drove to the toy **store. stores.**

story²

story¹ A **story** tells about people and places and what happens to them. **Stories** can be make-believe or true. Do you know the **story** about the three bears? **stories.**

story² In a building, a **story** is all the rooms on one floor. Matthew's house has two **stories. stories.**

sun

sun The **sun** is a hot ball of gas. It is very far away from the earth. The **sun** gives us heat and light. The earth goes around the **sun.**

T

tap Tap means to hit lightly. He **tapped** on the window. **tapped, tapping.**

tape I **Tape** is a long piece of paper, plastic, or some other material. Sticky **tape** is used to wrap things. 2 **Tape** also means to make a record on a special plastic **tape**. He **taped** the movie. **taped, taping.**

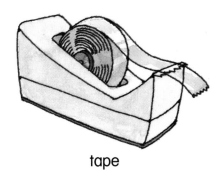

tape

teacher A **teacher** helps people learn. **Teachers** work in schools. **teachers.**

ten **Ten** is the number 10. **Ten** is one more than nine. **tens.**

that Who is the owner of **that** bike? I know **that** you are busy.

teacher

the What is **the** name of your dog? **The** cat Jamie found is black.

their **Their** dog is black and mine has spots.

then Dad used to go running, and he was very thin **then.** We went skating, and **then** we had hot chocolate.

they Luis and Elena came home late because **they** stopped to play.

those Megan bought **those** books. **Those** are her books and these are mine.

their

time

top¹

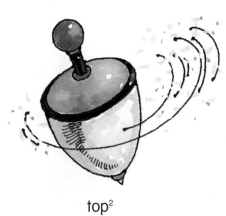

top²

three **Three** is the number 3. **Three** is one more than two. **threes.**

time **Time** is always going by. Seconds, minutes, hours, days, months, and years are ways we measure **time.** Clocks tell us what **time** it is.

to Are you going **to** the beach? What do you want **to** take?

too She felt **too** sad to go to the party. I was tired, and I was hungry **too.**

top¹ **Top** means the highest part. We saw the **top** of the mountain. **tops.**

top² A **top** is a toy that spins. The **top** went round and round. **tops.**

train A **train** is used to carry people and goods from one place to another. A **train** runs on a track and has many cars hooked together. An engine at the front makes the **train** go. **trains.**

tree A **tree** is a big plant. It has a trunk, branches, and leaves. Some **trees** have fruit that we eat. **trees.**

try **Try** means to set out to do something if you can. **Try** to hit the ball. **tried, trying.**

two **Two** is the number 2. **Two** is one more than one. **twos.**

U

up   The price of candy went **up.** The cat ran **up** the tree. We got **up** at seven o'clock. Your time is **up** now.

us   Many of **us** played outside after lunch. The teacher called **us** when it was time to come inside.

V

very   Jerry was **very** hungry. He had a **very** large dinner.

up

W

want   When you **want** something, you would like to have it or to do it. **I want** a kitten. **wanted, wanting.**

was   Her dog **was** gone. She **was** sad.

we   I met Latasha and **we** went skating.

went   Kerri **went** to the store.

were   They **were** cleaning the house. We **were** sorry it rained.

we

what   What is his name? Linda doesn't know **what** to do.

when   When are you leaving?

will   I **will** be able to go to the party. Sue **will** ask her mom to drive me.

with   Do you want to go **with** us? I cut the meat **with** a knife.

would   **Would** you like some candy? She said she **would** come to the party.

Y

yard   A **yard** is a piece of ground next to a house or a school. A **yard** may have a fence around it. Mother let us play outside, but we could not leave the **yard. yards.**

yard

yellow   **Yellow** is a color. Lemons and butter are **yellow.**

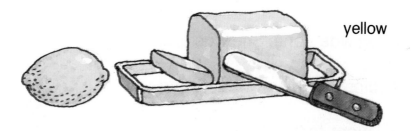

yellow

yes   When Ashley says **yes** to something, she wants to do it. When Kevin asked her to come over, she said, **"Yes."**

you   **You** have two sisters and I have one. **You** have more sisters than I do.

_____ 's

Word Place

Here is a place to keep words
you want to use again.
Put each word on the page
with the same beginning letter.

Handwriting Models

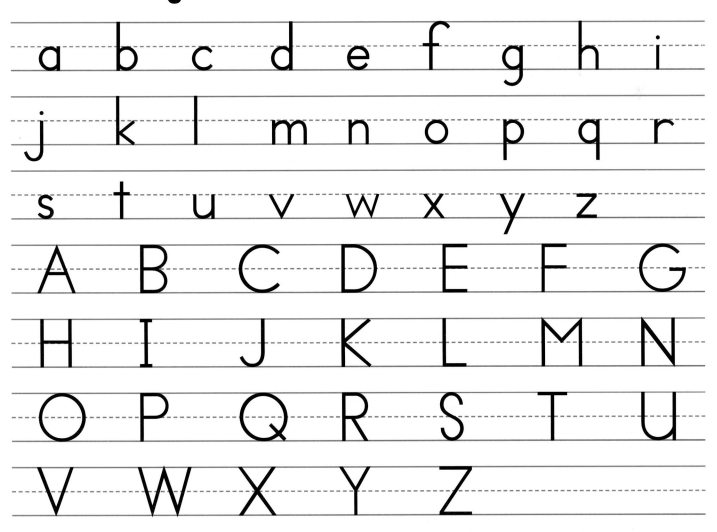

a b c d e f g h i
j k l m n o p q r
s t u v w x y z
A B C D E F G
H I J K L M N
O P Q R S T U
V W X Y Z

A a   B b

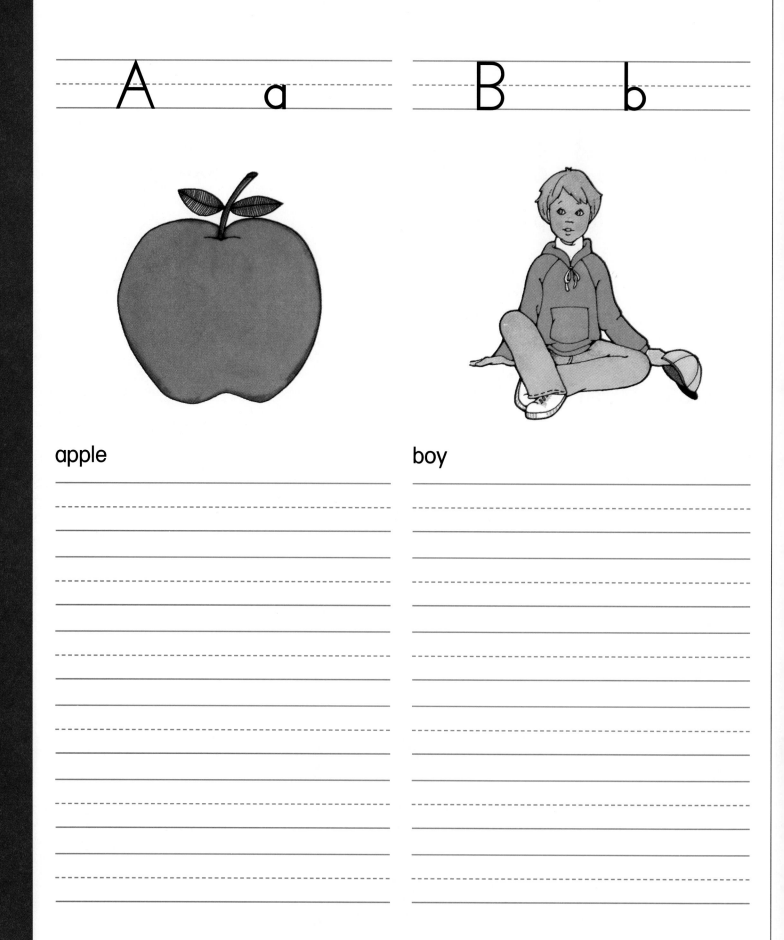

apple

boy

C c   D d

cat

dog

E e   F f

elephant

fish

G g　　H h

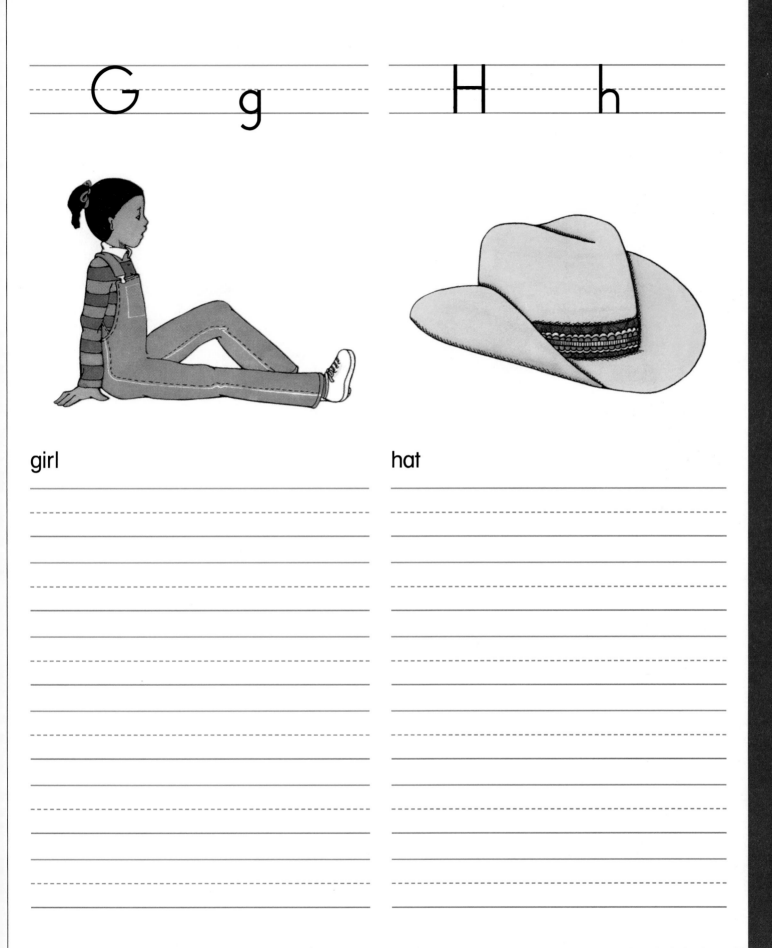

girl

hat

I i J j

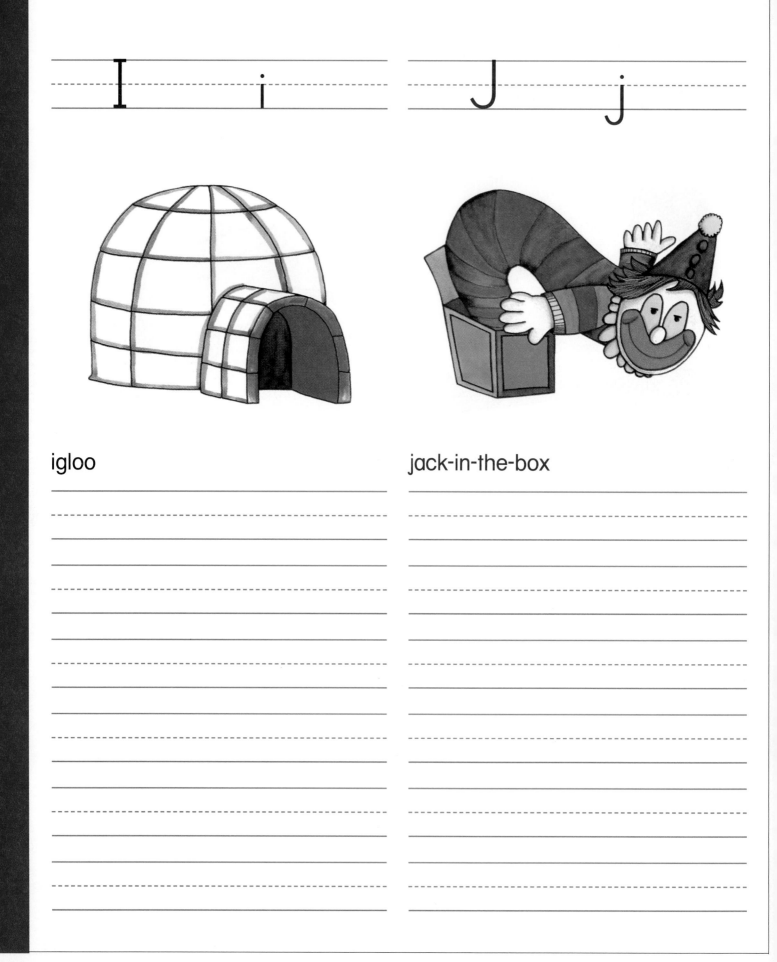

igloo

jack-in-the-box

K K k   L L l

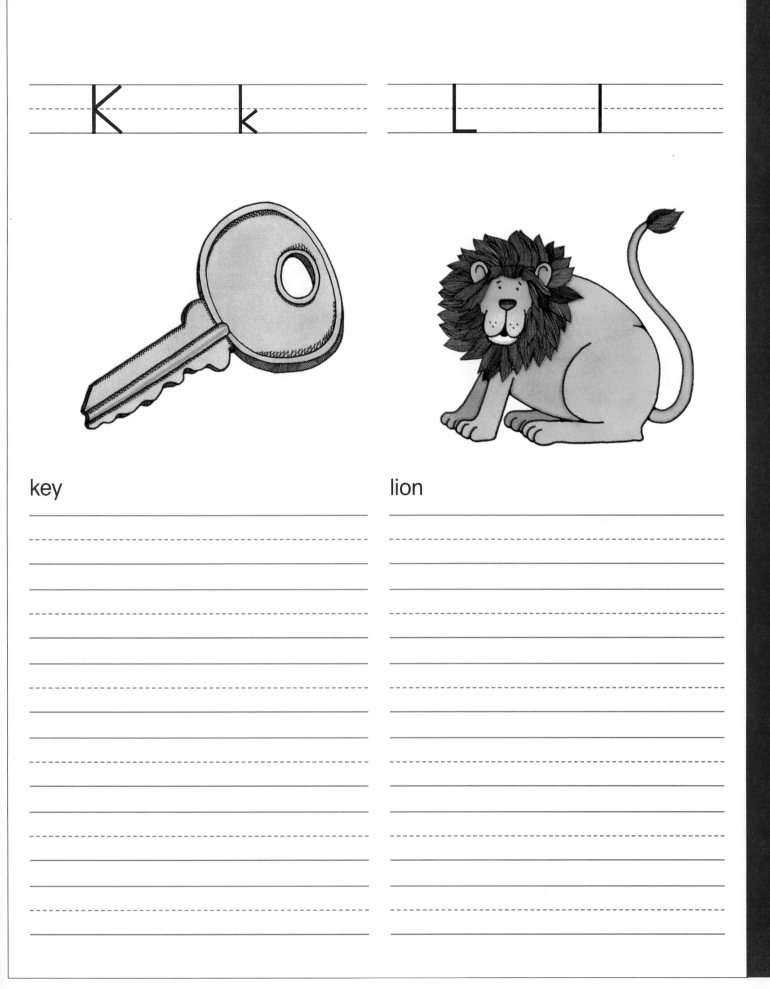

key

lion

M m   N n

moon

nest

O o

octopus

P p

puppet

Q q   R r

quarter

rabbit

S s   T t

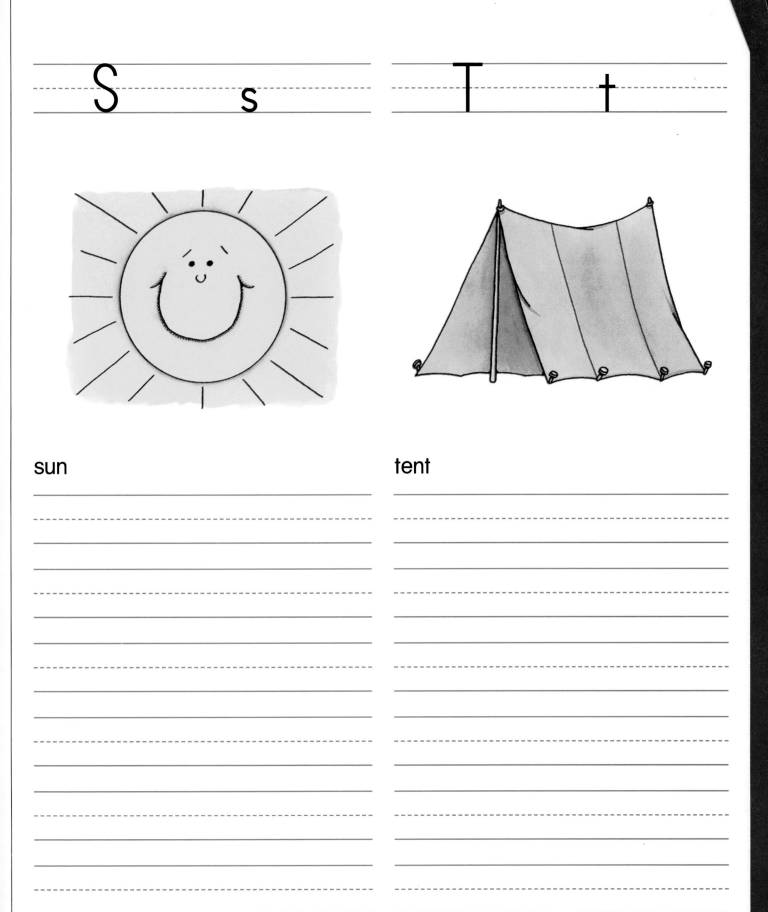

sun

tent

U u

V v

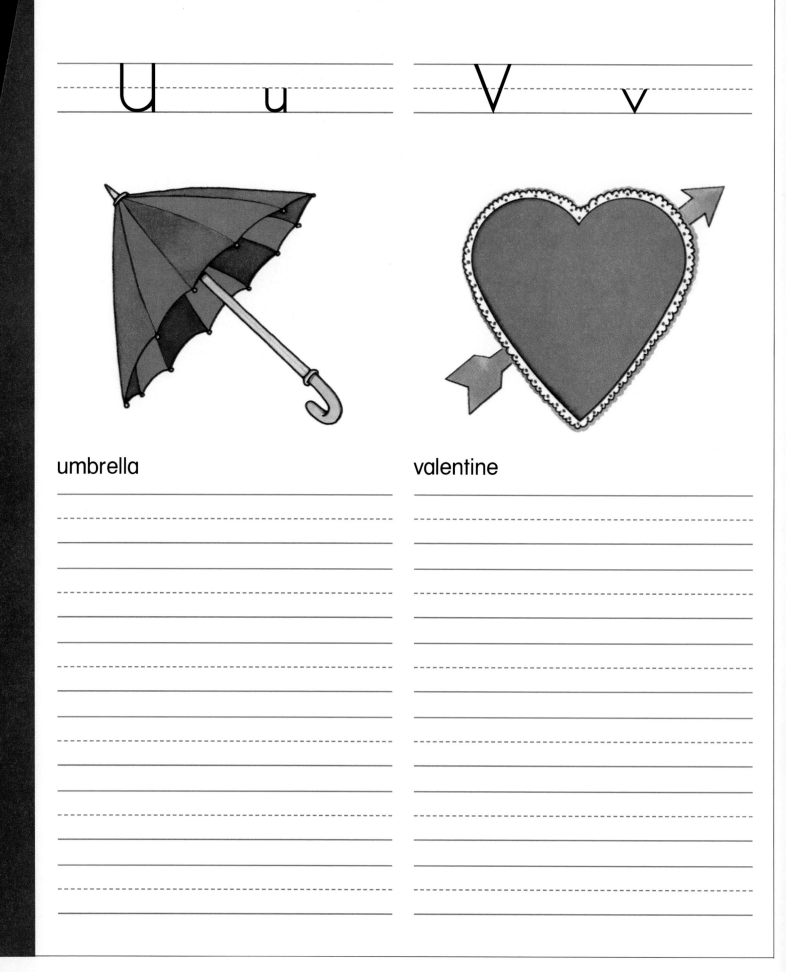

umbrella

valentine

W w

X x

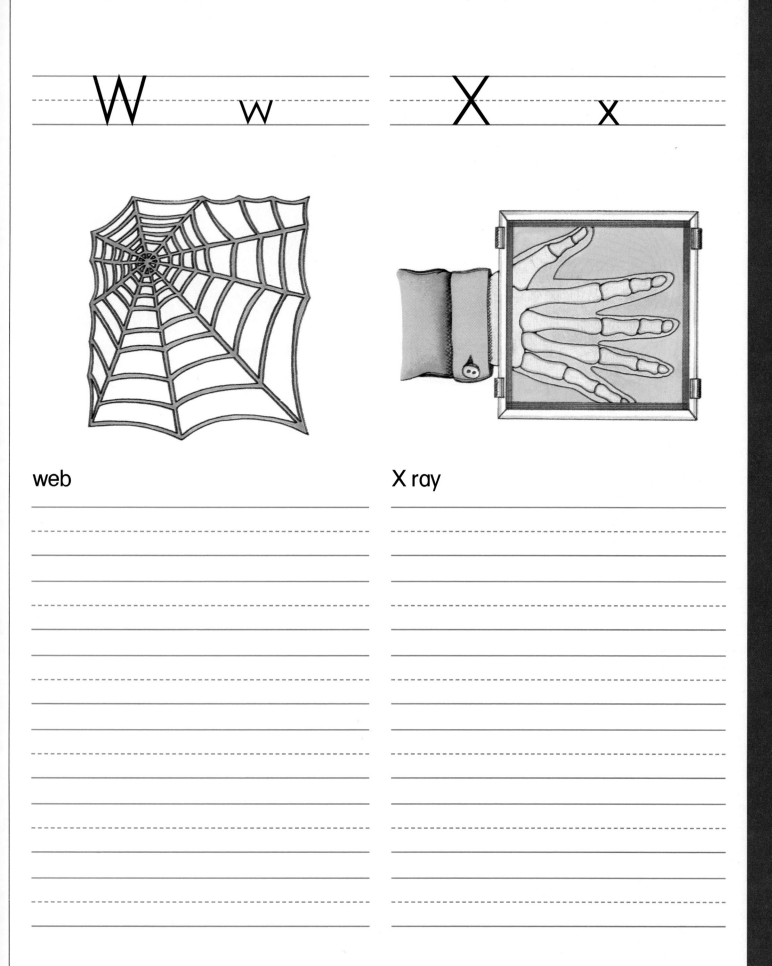

web

X ray

Y y
Z z

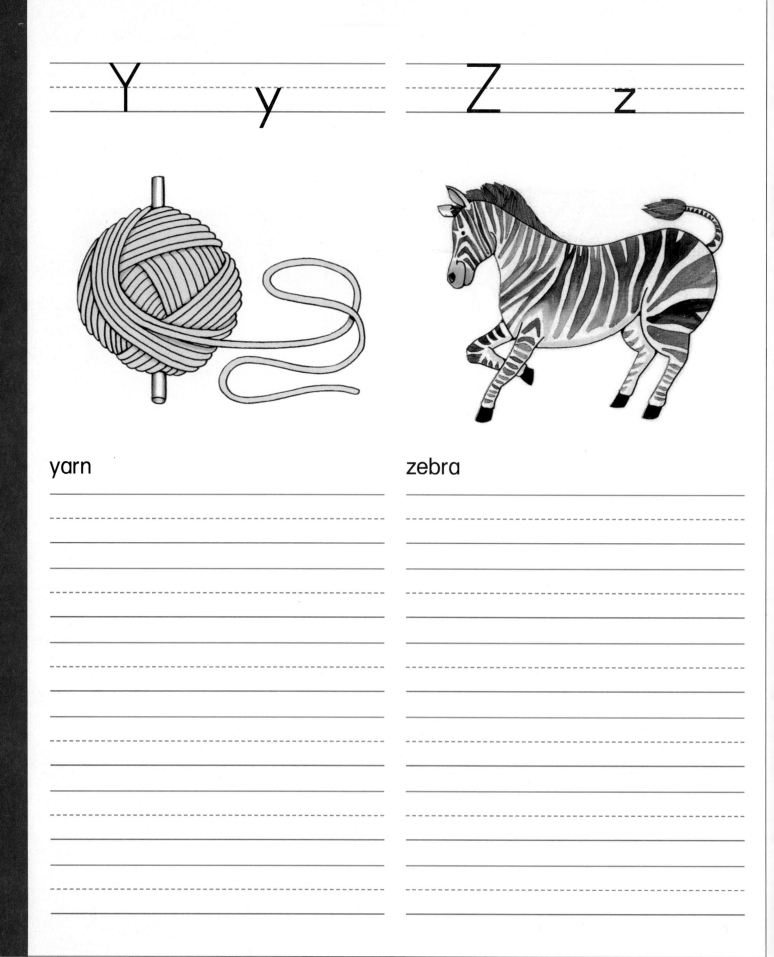

yarn

zebra